A
RIDICULOUS
MAN Donald Trump and the Verdict of History.

The distinguished English television interviewer Sir Michael Parkinson said in 2019 that 'no journalist worth their salt' would not want a sit-down interview with U.S. President Donald Trump 'and find out why he is such a ridiculous man. And I think you'd have to be equally ridiculous, in a sense, to try to imagine you might get something from him.' He said Mr Trump was 'impenetrable in his idiocy', adding 'He's a very dangerous man. And you feel sorry for America in that sense.'

A RIDICULOUS MAN

Donald Trump and the Verdict of History.

Norman Abjorensen

ARDEN

© Norman Abjorensen 2020

First published 2020 by
Australian Scholarly Publishing Pty Ltd
under its ARDEN international imprint

Australian Scholarly Publishing Pty Ltd
7 Lt Lothian St Nth, North Melbourne, Vic 3051
enquiry@scholarly.info / www.scholarly.info

ISBN 978-1-922454-02-7

Cover design: Sarah Anderson

For Carmel, who first asked the question.

Contents

Snapshot, November 2016
Politics goes punk[1]

The names Johnny Rotten and Donald Trump would not normally be found in the same sentence, but 40 years ago the Sex Pistols and other punk rockers were doing to popular music what Trump and other populist insurgents are now doing to politics – and the similarities are many.

The immediate point of comparison is in the full-frontal assault on the status quo that each represents: punk on the musical establishment and Trump on the political class. The assault was deliberately and provocatively transgressive in each case, seeking to maximise the impact through publicity and play to the gallery. If piercings in various parts of the body revolted many, there were more than a few who not only rejoiced in the shock value but emulated the effect; it was OK to look nasty. Trump's 'locker-room banter' offended many, but there were those among his followers who took it as an affirmation of their own mores.

With the rise of punk in the mid-1970s, musical ability no longer counted; it was simply not necessary to know how to play an instrument, as the hapless Sid Vicious, among others, showed. With Trump, it was irrelevant that he had never held elective office nor, in any sense at all had he been held accountable in the past. Experience was not only irrelevant, it was what the hated establishment thrived on.

Traditions, in each case, are not only ignored but

derided; there are no heroes to admire, only figures to tear down. Nothing from the past, however recent, is worth preserving; all can be remade according to new rules, not the old.

Punk rockers didn't ingratiate themselves with audiences; they sneered at them, shouted abuse and even spat at them – and the crowds called out for more. Trump would demean and exploit his audience by distorting reality with lies, exaggeration and hyperbole while he heaped scorn on the political elders of both sides, denigrating long and once hallowed traditions; he was cheered on to go even further.

Nothing to either punk or Trump was taboo: make fun of the monarchy, praise Hitler, mock the disabled, engage in racial and sexual vilification. There were no longer any barriers; bipartisanship was trucking with the hated establishment enemy; good manners were for the weak and subservient – and, of course, the political class.

In both the rise of punk and the advent of Trump, it is possible to discern a backlash effect – in each case a sense of pent-up resentment over perceived exclusion.

Punk arose as a musical genre (and cultural force) between 1974 and 1976, primarily in the United States, Britain and Australia, as a rejection of what was perceived as the excesses and over-sophistication of mainstream 1970s rock. It quickly spread elsewhere, even to the former Soviet Union.

The lavish orchestration of musicians like Rick Wakeman and the increasingly esoteric music of Pink Floyd had taken rock a long way from its three-chord, basic origins; the new music could not be danced to; it was seen as having little to do with the grit and toil of everyday life – just as Trump's legions found the new age, almost abstract, concerns of the Democratic Party ever more alien and disconnected from them.

The growing notoriety of punk rock in the UK was furthered by a televised incident that was widely publicised, and in many ways came to define the transgressive, public face of the phenomenon. Appearing on a London show called 'Thames Today,' guitarist Steve Jones of the Sex Pistols was provoked into a verbal altercation by the host, Bill Grundy, swearing at him on live television in gross violation of what were, at the time, accepted standards of propriety. The rules of what you could say in public had been torn up, just as Donald rewrote the manual on behaviour.

Punk bands typically performed frenetically-paced songs with hard-edged lyrics, simple repetitive chords and stripped-down instrumentation. The material was often overtly political and blatantly anti-establishment; the music was raw, abrasive and basic. Punk left no room for subtlety. Many punk bands also sought to bypass the mainstream industry by producing and even distributing their own records. Donald Trump, similarly, had no need for a political machine nor, as it turned out, even a political party once he had secured the Republican nomination.

The term punk was first used by some American critics in reference to garage bands and their followers, but later came to be applied to what increasingly looked like a new musical movement. Like the rise of Trump, it took some time for the groundswell to be noticed. Bands such as MC5, the Stooges and the New York Dolls heralded an emerging shift; the Sex Pistols, the Ramones and the Clash were in the vanguard. It soon spawned a distinctive punk subculture, as aggressive and sneering as the music and the bands performing it. The music magazine, *Punk*, which first appeared at the end of 1975 to cover the New York underground scene, popularised the term. Sociologists saw punk as the expression of post-industrial angst by disaffected working-class youth.

Punk's heyday was brief, but far from uneventful. By the early 1980s, it had lost its original appeal, but it left an indelible mark. Punk was, if anything, dynamic, and musicians identifying with or inspired by punk also experimented with a broad range of variations, giving rise to post-punk and the alternative rock movement. By the end of the 20th century, punk rock had been adopted by the mainstream, as pop punk and punk rock bands such as Green Day, Rancid, Sublime, the Offspring and Blink-182 brought the genre widespread popularity – and even respectability.

To what extent Trump and populism will follow the same path is hard to say – but whatever its longevity, in terms of both a movement and a presidency, its footprint will be with us for quite some time.

Music after punk was never quite the same again; the same might safely be said for politics post-Trump.

1.

The Historian's Challenge

Trump and his incipient regime are utterly abnormal.
– Sean Wilentz

'The historian's task is to present what actually happened', so begins an oft-quoted paper written in 1821 by the great Wilhelm von Humboldt.[2] Of course, that is but a starting point; the explanation – the ordering of facts, the construction of a cogent narrative, and the necessary contextualisation – is the part that attempts to make sense of what actually happened. But what if what actually happened makes little or no sense at all? How does one explain the seemingly inexplicable? What sort of history is it that a future reader will shake her head in utter disbelief, refusing to accept that the events so described actually happened?

How was it possible that a brash New York property developer and reality television host, devoid of any experience in public office or government at any level and with little knowledge of anything beyond his private business world, was suddenly elevated to the highest position in the most powerful nation in the history of the planet? How could a man who promised to run the country like a business be elected when hotels and casino businesses of his had declared bankruptcy six times between 1991 and 2009 because they could not meet commitments? How was it possible that a man who philanders with porn stars, buys their silence, and boasts about his sexual assaults on women, was able to attract votes from women and, even more incredulously, was supported by conservative Christians? How was it possible that a man who cheated his way out of military service could become commander-in-chief of the most powerful military force in history? How was it possible that such a demonstrably uncultured man, on whom education had had no discernible impact whatever, became the leader of a nation that is home to many of the world's finest universities, research organisations and cultural institutions? How was it possible that a man whose public discourse draws exclusively upon schoolyard taunts, gratuitous insults, and name-calling became the public face of the world's most powerful nation? How was it possible that a man who cannot help but respond with anger to every perceived slight, no matter how petty or trivial, be put in charge of a nuclear arsenal capable of destroying the planet many times over? How was it possible that a man who brazenly lies repeatedly and constantly could win the trust of a mighty nation (or at least the almost 63 million who voted for him in 2016)? How was it possible that a man could preside over a government constitutionally founded on the separation of powers and executive accountability when he himself so blatantly and disdainfully disregarded such constraints? How was it that a man could lead a nation ostensibly committed to promoting and defending human rights globally when he himself sympathises with neo-Nazis and white supremacists, constituting a key part of his 'base'? How did the Republican Party, long the bastion of the (mostly) respectable old-money establishment, fall under the sway of a swaggering mountebank of highly questionable character? How did a self-proclaimed billionaire, born into wealth and privilege and with a long history of complaining that wages were too high, attract support from the white working class? Such is the enormity of the challenge for the future historian of the Trump era.

And, almost certainly, there will be a demand for such a history. Infamy is a powerful attraction – and the never-ending studies of Adolf Hitler attest to this. Less infamous and perhaps worthier subjects of study pale in comparison to those whose very unorthodoxy is their primary characteristic, and the more outrageous they appear in the flouting of prevailing norms, the greater is the demand to know more – the what, the how and the why.

The classical historian, Anthony Bennett, pondered this question when he approached the subject of Caligula, noting the ongoing appetite for more despite a paucity of historical sources. Of all the emperors of ancient Rome, with the possible exception of Nero, none surpasses Caligula's reputation for infamy, he writes. Yet Nero had fourteen years to perfect his image against Caligula's modest four. Why the interest in Caligula when he held, as far as is known, no profound views on government nor represented any major historical trend?

His reign was exceptionally brief, shorter, for example than those of Galerius (six years), or Crispus (nine), or Licinius the First and the Second (twenty-three between them), emperors who have suffered general neglect and whose names remain obscure … There is, of course, a simple, immediate response to the question. Whether perversely or not, the literate reading public finds the life of Caligula interesting, while it stubbornly persists in showing little or no interest in Probus, Galerius or the like.[3]

In a similar vein, if infamy is the point of interest, it might well be that Trump's immediate predecessors will be similarly overshadowed despite their ostensibly stronger claims for serious historical study: Barack Obama in having become the first black president, and George W. Bush for his instigation of two costly wars in Iraq and Afghanistan.

Certainly, the historian of the future will not lack sources to consult regarding Trump, but the polarisation of public opinion is likely to be similar to that in the case of Caligula. Was he really so bad as some claim? To what extent were his defects and vices exaggerated by his political enemies? What, if any, were there mitigating circumstances that explain, or even counter, claims of his excesses?

To the ancient sources, Caligula was simply a destructive monster. The philosopher Seneca, seeking to ingratiate himself with Claudius, assured the emperor that his predecessor had 'wasted and utterly destroyed the empire'. Yet, as Barrett explains, this was patently untrue. The Roman provinces under his rule enjoyed stable and orderly government, the borders were secure, and tensions had eased with arch-rival Parthia. Many individual senators had prospered under Caligula, but that did not stop them from making 'desperate attempts' to doctor the record afterwards. Caligula, supposedly, cut a ridiculous figure insisting on personally leading his troops into battle, which no emperor had done in half a century. Yet, just two years after Caligula's death, Claudius repeated the feat, riding at the head of his army in Britain.

Caligula's excesses and incompetence supposedly left Rome bankrupt, but his successor found finances so healthy that he was able to abolish taxes and embark on large-scale building projects. Caligula, it was said, had the blood of the people on his hands, yet when he was assassinated the prevailing mood was one of anger. In one depiction of Caligula, he is said to have offered his foot to be kissed – an act striking at the very heart of Roman *gravitas* and *dignitas* – yet even Seneca, for all his bias, suggests this might have not been what happened, and that the emperor was only showing off his new slippers! But, as Bennett reminds us, Claudius found himself in a very precarious position, coming to power only because of Caligula's murder. It was in his interests to promote the idea that Caligula had died not because the imperial system was inherently evil but because Caligula was an inherently evil emperor.[4]

What changed?

In considering the case of Donald Trump, clearly there had been a shift in the political climate. What changed? Was it a sudden rupture or the culmination of a process of evolution? Was Trump the agent of change or merely the product of forces already in play? Who was he and where did he come from? These are the key questions.

It was not long after his election in 2016 that speculation began as to how future history might seek to explain what had happened. The author and commentator, David Frum, himself a Republican, surveyed in 2017 the first year in office, setting out briefly the issues with which a future historian would grapple. Frum noted how Trump had plunged the government which he led into chaos and disarray but serving all the while to enhance his own personal power. Trump had persuaded millions of Americans to ignore 'fake news' from a 'corrupt media' controlled by 'enemies of the people'. He had allowed foreign powers as well as local politicians to tamper with the integrity of the electoral process for his own benefit, and had demanded – like an absolutist despot – that high officials disregard the law in favour of personal loyalty to him.

He has alienated allies, appeased large enemies, and goaded small ones to the edge of war. He has brutally inflamed the ethnic and class divisions that empowered him in the first place. He has enriched himself in government in a way that disheartens every honest public official and invites dishonest ones to imitate him.[5]

On 5 September 2018, the *New York Times* published an essay under the by-line of 'a senior official in the Trump Administration', which described a state of chaos and instability in the White House and efforts to keep the president's impulses in check. In a subsequent book that elaborated on the essay, the anonymous author turned his or her attention to the way in which future historians would write about the administration which would be remembered as 'among the most tumultuous in American history' as they recorded 'the volatility of the president's decision-making' along with 'the internal struggles of a government forced to grapple with it'.

They will write that his advisors came to find him unfit for the job. He couldn't focus on governing, and he was prone to abuses of power, from ill-conceived schemes to punish his political rivals to a propensity for undermining vital American institutions. They will document how officials considered drastic – some might say desperate – measures to warn the American people.[6]

Early indications suggested history would not be kind to the 45th president. After his first year in office, a group of more than 170 scholars from the American Political Science Association released a survey which aims to calculate the 'greatness' of every U.S. president. Displacing James Buchanan, who plunged the nation into civil war, Trump debuted in last place, in what the *New York Times* characterised as 'a first draft of Trump's place in presidential history'.[7]

The survey graded Trump's first year on a report-card scale, giving him a 'D' in 'legislative accomplishments' and 'communicating with the public' (presumably thanks to his prolific Twitter use), and an 'F' in 'foreign policy leadership' and 'embodying institutional norms'. Overall, the grades averaged out to an 'F' for his first year in office.

To the distinguished historian of American democracy, Sean Wilentz, writing in 2017, understanding the current situation had to begin with the recognition that 'Trump and his incipient regime are utterly abnormal'. Trump, he noted, represented 'a sharp break in our national political history – something unlike anything America, in all of its turbulence, has seen before, his election the result of a fundamental collapse in our politics.'[8]

And this was just the start.

2.

Reality & Donald Trump: 'Are ye fantastical?'

What you're seeing and what you're reading is not what's happening. – Donald Trump

These are not normal times. – Dan Rather

Was Donald Trump real? He certainly made an effort to have us believe so, using the handle @ realDonaldTrump on his hard worked Twitter account. Yet why do we have difficulty accepting what we see and hear? Why does so much of the Trump presidency seem like improbable parody, a protracted satirical skit that looks like it has escaped from *Saturday Night Live* and taken up residence in the White House?

Just as Banquo in Shakespeare's *Macbeth* is confounded when confronted by the appearance of the witches speaking of strange prophesies, so too are we both puzzled and bewildered by the emergence of this curious figure of Donald Trump, blundering, blustering and stumbling around the world stage: 'I' th' name of truth, are ye fantastical, or that indeed Which outwardly ye show?'[9]

Were the witches actually human, as suggested by their appearance, asks Banquo, or were they rather creatures conjured up from imagination? Does this creature called Trump – a name immediately suggestive of the gimcrack and the false, as in 'trumpery' and 'trumped up' charges[10] – actually come from the same planet? The orange skin, yellow hair and the white eye sockets feed the imagination on possible other origins. The language spoken is awkward and seemingly rote-learned rather than acquired. How else can one account for such words as 'bigly'? The creature, both in appearance and manner is, indeed, fantastical.

Fantastical or not, Donald Trump certainly inhabits a parallel universe, a place where he alone is the arbiter of reality. His appropriation of the hitherto perfectly useful designation, 'fake news', is a case in point. According to the First Draft News website,[11] there are seven types of fake news: satire or parody (no intention to cause harm but has potential to fool); false connection (when headlines, visuals or captions don't support the content); misleading content (misleading use of information to frame an issue or an individual); false context (when genuine content is shared with false contextual information); impostor content (when genuine sources are impersonated with false, made-up sources); manipulated content (when genuine information or imagery is manipulated to deceive, as with a 'doctored' photo); and fabricated content (new content is 100% false, designed to deceive and do harm).

But Trump, who has done more than anyone to popularise the term fake news, has no time for any of these nuanced distinctions: by his own definition, fake news is simply news with which he disagrees

– that is, negative (or insufficiently laudatory) coverage of Donald Trump. The distinguished Yale historian, Timothy Snyder, has identified ominous signs in Trump's violent rhetoric towards the media, writing: 'Like Hitler, the president used the word *lies* to mean statements of fact not to his liking, and presented journalism as a campaign against himself.'[12]

The arbiter of reality

Donald Trump's almost surreal campaign to lead the most powerful nation in the world was accompanied by a rhetoric which brought into being a new term: post-truth. The Oxford dictionary named post-truth its word of the year in 2016, and defined it as 'circumstances in which objective facts are less influential in shaping public opinion than appeals to emotion and personal belief'.

To be fair, Trump was not the first leader to quibble with reality. The earlier presidency of George W. Bush (2001–9) had its own issues when confronted with unpalatable facts. Under the Bush administration, the term 'reality-based community' was formed, attributed by journalist Ron Suskind to an unnamed official (believed to have been senior adviser Karl Rove, but he denied it) who used it to denigrate a critic of the administration's policies as someone who based their judgements on facts. Suskind wrote:

> The aide said that guys like me were 'in what we call the reality-based community', which he defined as people who 'believe that solutions emerge from your judicious study of discernible reality'. [...] 'That's not the way the world really works anymore', he continued. 'We're an empire now,

and when we act, we create our own reality. And while you're studying that reality – judiciously, as you will – we'll act again, creating other new realities, which you can study too, and that's how things will sort out. We're history's actors...and you, all of you, will be left to just study what we do.'[13]

Trump, however, just took it to a new level.

Trump's antagonism towards traditional journalism of checking facts and reporting objectively quickly became apparent once in office. Long known for his scant regard for the truth and his propensity for exaggeration – his ghost writer having revealed how gleefully he revelled in the term 'truthful hyperbole' as an effective means of promotion in his 1987 book *Trump: The Art of the Deal*[14] – the newly-installed president took issue with the reporting of crowd size at his inauguration when news media suggested it was smaller than that of his predecessor, Barack Obama. His press secretary, Sean Spicer, accused the media of deliberately underestimating the size of the crowd, and stated that the ceremony had drawn the 'largest audience to ever witness an inauguration – period – both in person and around the globe'.[15] Comparable photographs showed this was demonstrably false.[16]

Next day, Trump's campaign strategist and counsellor, Kellyanne Conway, sought to defend Spicer's statements in an interview, observing that he had given what she infamously termed 'alternative facts.' Interrupted by the interviewer with the statement that so-called 'alternative facts' amounted to falsehoods, Conway stood her ground, arguing that crowd numbers in general could not be assessed with certainty. Conway later defended her choice of words, defining 'alternative facts' as 'additional facts and alternative information'. It quickly established the new administration's tenuous relationship with reality.[17]

The respected journalist Dan Rather, a veteran of the political beat, was aghast, taking to social media, with a grim warning:

> These are not normal times. These are extraordinary times. And extraordinary times call for extraordinary measures. When you have a spokesperson for the president of the United States wrap up a lie in the Orwellian phrase 'alternative facts'...When you have a press secretary in his first appearance before the White House reporters threaten, bully, lie, and then walk out of the briefing room without the cojones to answer a single question...Facts and the truth are not partisan. They are the bedrock of our democracy. And you are either with them, with us, with our Constitution, our history, and the future of our nation, or you are against it. Everyone must answer that question.[18]

It was not only Rather who saw shades of George Orwell's dystopian 1949 novel, *Nineteen Eighty-Four*, in the chilling words emanating from the White House, with its suggestions of 'newspeak' and 'doublethink'.

'Newspeak', as Orwell wrote in an appendix to the novel, follows most of the rules of English grammar, yet is a language characterised by a continually diminishing vocabulary; complete thoughts reduced to simple terms of simplistic meaning. Its aim is to serve the ideology of the government by limiting freedom of thought. For 'doublethink', Orwell drew on examples from Soviet totalitarianism to describe a process of indoctrination that requires the subject to accept as true that which is clearly false, or to simultaneously accept two mutually contradictory beliefs as correct, often in contravention to one's own memories or sense of reality. It is essentially a form of epistemological nihilism.

Former *New York Times* executive editor, Jill Abramson, also drew the Orwell comparison, adding: 'Alternative facts are just lies'.[19] Many members of the general public also turned to Orwell for confirmation, sending the book back into the best-seller lists and the publisher ordering a reprint run of 75,000.[20]

More than three years later, in June, 2020 – after fact-checking Trump had become a key feature of much of the mainstream media, much to his anger – the president and his advisers engaged in another battle with reality, in what was probably a first: threatening a news organisation with legal action over an opinion poll with which the president took exception. The CNN television network had published a poll five months out from the election showing Trump trailing his Democratic opponent, Joe Biden.

'It's a stunt and a phony poll to cause voter suppression, stifle momentum and enthusiasm for the President, and present a false view generally of the actual support across America for the President', read the letter, signed by the Trump campaign's senior legal adviser Jenna Ellis and chief operating officer Michael Glassner. The campaign formally requested that CNN retract the poll and publish a 'full, fair, and conspicuous retraction, apology, and clarification to correct its misleading conclusions'. CNN told the campaign that its 'allegations and demands are rejected in their entirety'.[21]

Trump's self-appointed role as the sole arbiter of

reality comes at a high cost, Tom Nichols wrote in *The Atlantic*, noting that in Trump's world, reality, like everything else, is negotiable. Trump and his enablers had managed to achieve something even more dangerous than trying to run a government just on gut feeling and conspiracy theories: by attacking sources of authoritative knowledge beyond the president himself, inoculated a huge swath of the American public against ever being informed about anything, providing millions of Americans with a resistance to learning that would long outlive his administration.

From vaccines to trade wars to nuclear arms, Trump claimed that he knew better than anyone else, a fantasy encouraged and fed by his staff. Nichols quotes the president's trade adviser, Peter Navarro: 'My function, really, as an economist is to try to provide the underlying analytics that confirm his intuition. And his intuition is always right in these matters.'[22]

So much for expertise; it has been replaced by sycophancy.

Trump as spectacle

Seeking, as the future historian must, to locate Donald Trump within a recognisable context of something approximating reality, presents significant difficulties. Trump's own relationship with truth of any kind is tenuous at best. When the president was worried that he might become the subject of investigation by former FBI director Robert Mueller looking at Russian interference in the 2016 election, Trump's immediate reaction was a desire to talk to the investigators – a suggestion promptly rejected by his legal team. They were acutely aware, as were long-time friends and close advisers, of his tendency to disconnect from facts and remember experiences the way it suited him at the moment. Indeed, as Philip Rucker and Carol Leonnig put in bluntly in *A Very Stable Genius: Donald J. Trump's Testing of America*: Lying has been part of Trump's act all his life.[23]

The use of the word 'act' here is telling. Is this nothing more than elaborate performance? Is the choreographed projection of Donald J. Trump merely a sideshow attraction? Or does it reflect – or even distract from – an underlying reality (assuming such a reality even exists)? What will the historian find when sifting through all this?

Even the man himself, not usually credited with a high degree of self-awareness, concedes Donald Trump is, first and foremost, a performance. A long-time acquaintance, Anthony Scaramucci, who worked (very) briefly as the president's communications director, recalled having once put the question to Trump: 'Are you an act?' Trump responded: 'I'm a total act and I don't understand why people don't get it.'[24] Of course, as is patently obvious, admitting to be an 'act' is part of the act.

The act has a long history. In 1990, Trump first alluded to it in an interview with *Playboy*, when he was asked what all the glitz – the yacht, the bronze tower, the casinos – really meant to him. He replied: 'Props for the show.'

And what is the show?
The show is Trump and it is sold-out performances everywhere. I've had fun doing it and will continue to have fun, and I think most people enjoy it.

Do you think the ones who hate it are jealous?

They could be whatever – but the vast majority
dig it.[25]

A number of scholars have accepted the
contemporary challenge offered by Trump as an
example of late capitalism's preferencing of style
over content: Trump considered as spectacle. One
such study seeks to explain Trump's rise through the
Republican nomination process and eventual election
as president in terms of the spectacle of entertainment
that was the hallmark of his campaign.[26] Drawing on
cultural anthropology, linguistic anthropology, and
rhetorical theory, the authors consider how Trump
elevates his entertainment value by crafting comedic
representations of his political opponents as well
as himself, with these representations taking the
form of a kind of embodied performance. It was not
just the white rural underclass who were attracted
to it, and not just conservatives, 'but also ... the
public at large, even those who strongly oppose
his candidacy. Whether understood as pleasing or
offensive, Trump's ongoing show was compelling.'
The authors emphasise the importance of
considering the specifics of Trump's entertainment
value – that is, 'how Trump's comedic media
appearances' over the course of the Republican
primary season 'built momentum in a celebrity and
mediatized culture'.
While Trump's unorthodox style appeared novel
in 2016, the study notes how other scholars in a
variety of fields have considered entertainment as
a value by positioning it as key to comprehending
class relations. For example, there was the use of
entertainers such as ballad singers, jugglers, puppet
masters, and comedians among the peasantry in
the sixteenth through eighteenth centuries. It cites

the work of historian Peter Burke[27] who notes that these performers, by attracting the attention of audiences from across the class spectrum, enabled mutual permeability between elite and popular culture. Similarly, philosopher and literary critic Mikhail Bakhtin's writings[28] on the French Renaissance novelist Rabelais illuminate the power of carnivalesque entertainment: fools and clowns subverting the social order through acts of parody, poking vulgar fun at the mystique of political rulers and stirring rebellion in their audiences. Humorous performance, the authors note, citing Erving Goffman,[29] is protected from the scrutiny that would be applied in other discursive domains.

But is there anything behind the spectacle? Is there anything more to Donald J. Trump than this projected construct, this artifice? Psychology professor Dan P. McAdams, author of *The Strange Case of Donald J. Trump: A Psychological Reckoning*,[30] addressed these very same questions: Who, really, is Donald Trump? What's behind the actor's mask?

McAdams wrote in an article just before Trump won the 2016 election that he could discern little more than 'narcissistic motivations and a complementary personal narrative' about winning at any cost. He added:

> It is as if Trump has invested so much of himself in developing and refining his socially dominant role that he has nothing left over to create a meaningful story for his life, or for the nation. *It is always Donald Trump playing Donald Trump*, fighting to win, but never knowing why.[31]

To television critic James Poniewozik, the key to understanding Trump lies in acknowledging first and foremost that he became known as a reality television performer, and trying to understand him as a person with psychology and strategy and motivation will inevitably spiral into confusion. The key was to remember that 'Donald Trump is not a person. He's a TV character.' If you want to understand what President Trump would do in any situation, then, it's more helpful to ask: What would TV do? What does TV want? Poniewozik writes: 'It wants conflict. It wants excitement. If there is something that can blow up, it should blow up. It wants a fight. It wants *more*. It is always eating and never full.'[32]

'What's this all about?'

Another problem for the historian is convincingly explaining how a man displaying such abysmal ignorance of nearly everything became leader of the mightiest nation on earth. Surely, a future reader will ask when presented with the historian's findings, this cannot be so. Is this a parody? Is this merely caricature? It makes no sense at all.

In late 2019, *Time* magazine looked at the revelations of ignorance over the three years since the election and noted that of all the gambles in electing the most politically inexperienced candidate ever to the highest elected office in the world, the danger of ignorance may prove the greatest of them all. 'What Donald Trump "knows" derives from the seamy worlds of real estate, casinos and reality TV, and it is his infected worldview, paired with his distant acquaintance with actual truth, that is now the most frightening characteristic of this presidency.'[33]

Trump appeared to live in a perpetual present,

and if there was a past he had no knowledge of it nor, apparently, any curiosity about it. One glaring example was Pearl Harbour – a name that almost every school student in the world would know as not just a place name but a significant event in the history of the 20th century, when the Japanese mounted a surprise attack on the US naval base in Hawaii in 1941. Certainly, every American child would connect the name with a seminal event in their own history – but not Donald Trump.

Setting out on his first visit to Asia, the presidential entourage touched down in Hawaii to refuel and break up the long trip. It had been arranged for the president and the First Lady to make a pilgrimage to the memorial at Pearl Harbour for the 2,300 American service personnel who died in the attack. The plan was to take a private tour of the USS *Arizona* Memorial just off the coast of Honolulu where it straddles the hull of the battleship that sank during the attack. As the party travelled by boat to the stark white memorial, the president took aside his chief of staff, former marines general, John Kelly, and asked him: 'Hey, John, what's this all about? What's this a tour of?' As Philip Rucker and Carol Leonnig recount it:

Kelly was momentarily stunned. Trump had heard the phrase 'Pearl Harbour' and appeared to understand that he was visiting the scene of a historic battle but did not seem to know much else. Kelly explained to him that the stealth Japanese attack here had devastated the U.S. Pacific Fleet and prompted the country's entrance into World War II, eventually leading the United States to drop atom bombs on Japan. If Trump had learned about 'a date that will live in infamy' in school, it hadn't really pierced his consciousness or stuck with him.[34]

In a classic understatement, a former senior adviser is quoted by the authors as saying that Trump was 'at times dangerously uninformed'.

Trump's lack of historical knowledge was on display to foreign audiences as well. Meeting with France's president, Emmanuel Macron, at the United Nations in September 2017, Trump complimented him on the spectacular Bastille Day military parade they had watched together in Paris that summer. Trump told Macron he did not realise until seeing that parade that France had such a rich history of military conquest. He told an undoubtedly incredulous Macron that: 'You know, I really didn't know, but the French have won a lot of battles. I didn't know.'[35]

History and geography were not the only lowlights in the president's startling lack of knowledge. One struggles to comprehend his understanding (if any) of the wider neighbourhood in an extraordinary tweet in 2019 on the subject space exploration:

> For all of the money we are spending, NASA should NOT be talking about going to the Moon – We did that 50 years ago. They should be focused on the much bigger things we are doing, including Mars (of which the Moon is a part), Defense and Science![36]

The moon part of Mars? From which planet does that appear to be the case?

On Planet Trump

The view from Planet Trump is very different. So, too, for that matter, is Planet Trump itself. It cannot be seen through a conventional telescope; it exists in a separate reality altogether. It is a very small place, contained entirely inside the head of a single man, but like a cosmic light show, it is projected onto the entire world.

On this planet, Donald Trump is not only adored; he is worshipped. Elections have been abandoned as a grateful people have asked him to stay on forever. His approval ratings are close to 100 per cent. The mainstream media, such as the *New York Times* and *Washington Post*, routinely carry laudatory front-pages pieces on him, and his speeches are printed in full, discussed by academics and studied in schools. Every night, on prime-time television, America sits, watches and listens, hanging on every word, nodding in approval. *Time* magazine now has him permanently on the cover. Foreign leaders are forever calling him to offer praise in his handling of crises such as the coronavirus and to congratulate him on winning yet another Nobel Peace Prize.

In the actually existing United States, Mount Rushmore National Memorial is a massive sculpture carved into Mount Rushmore in the Black Hills region of South Dakota, depicting the most revered presidents George Washington, Thomas Jefferson, Theodore Roosevelt and Abraham Lincoln. But on Planet Trump, plans are under way to add a fifth – Donald J. Trump. According to multiple media reports, a White House aide in 2019 contacted South Dakota governor, Kristi Noem, to inquire about possibly adding Trump's face to the landmark. At an earlier meeting in the White House, when Noem was a congresswoman, Trump had raised the question with her. 'He said, 'Kristi, come on over here. Shake my hand', she said. 'I shook his hand, and I said, 'Mr. President, you should come to South Dakota sometime. We have Mount Rushmore.'

And he goes, 'Do you know it's my dream to have my face on Mount Rushmore?" Noem said she started laughing. 'He wasn't laughing', she said. 'So, he was totally serious.'[37]

Trump on Mount Rushmore? Only on Planet Trump.

Of course, it wasn't always like this. In the bad old days, before Planet Trump was widely known, those enemies of the people, journalists and the like, had the temerity to argue that there was no such place; they even took it on to fact-check the president every time he sought to show the way to this enlightened place. They even called him a liar for talking about it.

As of 3 April 2020, the *Washington Post* and its team of fact-checkers had determined that in President Trump's 1,170 days of his presidency, he had made 18,000 false or misleading statements. That works out to an average of 15.38 lies per day while he's been in office. 'He lies with such frequency that he is in a category separate from most of us', observed psychologist Christian Hart who had made a study of lying, noting that Trump's propensity to lie far exceeded that of any other politician.[38] Writing about the work of the fact checkers, one commentator concluded:

The president is a bold, intentional liar, by any moral definition. A habitual liar. A blatant liar. An instinctual liar. A reckless liar. An ignorant liar. A pathological liar. A hopeless liar. A gratuitous liar. A malevolent liar.[39]

But how fair is this? If to lie is to intentionally deceive by distorting, contradicting or denying the truth, is it lying if you really believe that the lie you are speaking is true? It might well be that here we have a case on Planet Trump where reality is just what you say it is, and because you say it, then it is real, it is true. You actually conjure into existence something just by saying it. Trump won the popular vote. Bingo! So he did. Two million more people attended the inauguration than what was reported. Presto! They materialise.

A case in point is the coronavirus pandemic crisis that arose in 2020. It might have devastated the United States leaving hundreds of thousands of Americans dead, but on Planet Trump it was but a minor irritation, as tracked by *The Atlantic*. In February, as the first cases of COVID-19 began to appear, Trump was adamant that the virus would weaken 'when we get into April, in the warmer weather – that has a very negative effect on that, and that type of a virus', and that the outbreak would be temporary: 'It's going to disappear. One day it's like a miracle – it will disappear.' In June, the pandemic is 'fading away. It's going to fade away'; in July, it was 'getting under control'. A claim made on multiple occasions was that cases 'are going up in the U.S. because we are testing far more than any other country'. That might have been the case on Planet Trump but, in fact, COVID-19 cases were not rising because of 'our big-number testing'. Outside the Northeast, the share of tests conducted that came back positive was increasing, with the sharpest spike happening in southern states. In some states, such as Arizona and Florida, the number of new cases being reported was outpacing any increase in the states' testing ability. And as states set new daily case records and report increasing hospitalizations, all signs pointed to a worsening crisis. [40]

Perhaps the most telling episode in the handling of the coronavirus crisis was Donald Trump's address to a campaign rally in June in Tulsa, Oklahoma, that he had asked officials to slow down testing for COVID-19 because case numbers in the country were rising so rapidly. Using racist language, Trump referring to the virus as 'kung flu', and described testing for the virus as a 'double-edged sword' because it led to the identification of more cases. By that time, the U. S. had tested 25 million people, far more than other countries, Trump said, adding: 'When you do testing to that extent, you're gonna find more people, you're gonna find more cases. So I said to my people slow the testing down.' A White House official later said that Trump was joking.[41] But few believed it was a joke. Paul Krugman wrote in the *New York Times* that it was entirely consistent with efforts by the Trump team in trying to suppress bad news about the pandemic; a case of 'what you don't know can't hurt Trump'.[42]

Here was a veritable window right into the strange reality-defying world of Planet Trump. If you don't look, you don't find. If you don't test, you don't find cases. Problem solved. Crime would be so easy to eradicate on such a planet; you just stop investigating. Simple.

The greatest danger with one man's delusional world of fantasy is when it collides with the world of reality and other people are drawn into it, often unwittingly. When the fantasist is the most powerful man in the world you have trouble. The Ukraine scandal, which led to Trump's impeachment, provides a salutary lesson; it was, Nancy Gibbs wrote in *Time*, 'something even more alarming than a president who lies'.[43]

In his phone call with Ukrainian President Volodymyr Zelensky, in which he asked for a favour in return for military aid, Gibbs asked what reason would Trump have for raising 'a discredited fever swamp conspiracy theory about Crowdstrike' and the Democratic National Committee server being stashed somewhere in Ukraine unless he actually believed this to be true and worth pursuing?

He had every reason to think this was a private call; he wasn't shaping public opinion, rallying his base, tossing a new shiny object in front of reporters to chase. His hunger for dirt on Hunter Biden sounds like familiar, amoral, gutter politics. But he also pressured a foreign leader to enter his alternative universe. This is altogether different.

Planet Trump is a very different, and also very dangerous, place.

3.

The Ugly American

I know of nothing more despicable and pathetic than a man who devotes all the hours of the waking day to the making of money for money's sake. – John D. Rockefeller

The business of America is business. – Calvin Coolidge

I'll keep it short and sweet. Family, religion, friendship: These are the three demons you must slay if you wish to succeed in business. – C. Montgomery Burns

Where the fuck is the money? – Donald J. Trump

It would be comforting if Donald Trump were merely a cartoon character, nothing more than another caricature in the long-established genre depicting a stereotypical Ugly American, often characterised in popular culture by the tourists who 'arrive at a foreign destination demanding that others speak English and attend to their needs, all the while making a loud and garish spectacle of themselves.'[44] Alas, he is not. He is, in combination, all of those brash, swaggering, arrogant figures that have punctuated American history, even before the term gained currency from the title of the 1958 novel by Eugene Burdick and William Lederer that depicts the failures of the U.S. diplomatic corps in Southeast Asia. From the 19th century robber barons and the shameless stunt-pulling showman P. T. Barnum, through the political thugs like Chicago's Mayor

Daley and the infamous Joe McCarthy, the bully J. Edgar Hoover, the ruthless newspaper tycoon William Randolph Hearst ('Citizen Kane'), the segregationists like George Wallace, the tennis brats like John McEnroe, boxer Mike Tyson, any number of the Wall Street hucksters as portrayed by the fictitious Gordon Gecko, to Walt Disney's money-obsessed Uncle Scrooge and the rapacious Mr Burns of *The Simpsons*: Trump is all of these – and more. None of the others occupied such an exalted office; none wielded such immense power. The ugliness of Trump is magnified many times over.

Wide-eyed and witless, a newly-elected President Trump was unleashed on the world. Seasoned diplomats had encountered ignorant Americans and insular Americans, but they were totally unprepared for a man who knew so little about the world and cared even less. 'I never knew we had so many countries', the innocent abroad blurted out to Japanese officials at the Akasaka Palace in Tokyo during the first leg of a five-country visit to Asia a year after his election. The context was a reference to his first meeting with Japanese prime minister Shinzo Abe just days after his election, with Trump explaining that his relationship 'got off to quite a rocky start because I never ran for office, and here I am'. He continued: 'But I never ran, so I wasn't very experienced. And after I had won, everybody was calling me from all over the world. I never knew we had so many countries … I didn't know you were supposed to not see world leaders until after you were in office which was January 20th'.[45]

The gaffes came thick and fast, revealing a man of no learning and utterly devoid of intellectual curiosity; and they also came heavily laced with embarrassment. In the heady hours after it became clear that Trump had scored an unlikely victory, his transition team scrambled to provide details on the protocol for discussions with foreign leaders and the order in which they should be made. Before any of them could be made, however, the president of Egypt called Trump Tower and was put through to the president-elect. Taken by surprise, a nonplussed Trump mumbled into the phone: 'I love the Bangles! You know that song "Walk Like an Egyptian?"';[46] it was a reference to a hit by a 1980s pop group. The Egyptian president's response is not known.

Trump's first Secretary of State, Rex Tillerson, had worked hard to improve relations with India which he saw as a key ally against an expansionist China in the region. His developing relationship with Indian prime minister Narendra Modi led to a visit to India by Trump in November 2017. On 13 November, Trump sat down at a meeting with Modi – an event in which Tillerson had invested heavily and had high hopes for despite Trump's having, back at the White House, mocked Modi while affecting a fake Indian accent.

Trump, as usual, appeared not to have read the detailed briefing material prepared for him, and veered away from the main agenda item, which deeply concerned Modi – that of security, and especially the threats that India faced from Afghanistan, China, and Pakistan. Modi sought to refocus the discussion, raising his concerns about China's ambitions in the region. Trump at once revealed a breathtaking ignorance about geography, saying as he appeared to dismiss the threat to India: 'It's not like you've got China on your border.'[47] For the record, and as many school students would know, the two countries share one of the world's longest land borders, of 3,380 km. According to reports, Trump, while studying a briefing map of South Asia ahead of that 2017 meeting, expressed surprise at the existence of two small countries, mispronouncing Nepal as 'nipple' and laughingly referring to Bhutan as 'button'.[48]

Trump's problems with geography had a long history. While a candidate, he told a rally in Atlanta, Georgia, that 'Belgium is a beautiful city', after having said earlier that Brussels, the capital of the country, Belgium, was a 'hellhole' because of the lack of 'assimilation' of the Muslim population.[49] Even as president, according to former National Security Advisor John Bolton, he had asked if Finland was part of Russia and if Venezuela was part of the United States.[50]

International perceptions

Certainly, international perceptions of the United States changed under Trump's presidency. As had been the case throughout his presidency, Trump received largely negative reviews from publics around the world. Across 32 countries surveyed in 2019 by Pew Research Center,[51] a median of 64% said they did not have confidence in Trump to do the right thing in world affairs, while just 29% expressed confidence in the American leader.

According to the survey, anti-Trump sentiments were especially common in Western Europe: around three-in-four or more lacked confidence in Trump in Germany, Sweden, France, Spain and the Netherlands. He also got especially poor reviews in Mexico, where 89% did not have confidence in him. In nearly all nations where trends were available, Trump received lower ratings than his predecessor, Barack Obama.

A researcher at the University of Sydney, Brendon O'Connor, began investigating negative stereotyping of Americans, writing that 'Trump is the gift that keeps on giving for the project'. His research, based on analysing more than a hundred travel books written by Europeans from the early 19th century, showed that six dominant stereotypes about Americans were constructed in the 1820s and 1830s, and have persisted ever since.

These were: that American manners were extremely deficient; that Americans were often anti-intellectual, uncultured, and ignorant; that Americans lived ultimately bland lives; that Americans were particularly prone to boasting and annoying patriotism; that Americans were money obsessed and financially untrustworthy; and finally that Americans were hypocrites. Trump, for many, is the embodiment of these negative national stereotype.[52]

Noting polls, such as the Pew survey, O'Connor writes that, while there is widespread disapproval of Trump's nationalist, protectionist and racist policies, it is his persona that most repels non-Americans. 'Trump is strongly disliked across the world because he is the archetypal "ugly American": obnoxious, uncouth, boastful, materialistic, and duplicitous.'

'I am very rich'

Home-grown caricatures of the Ugly American permeate popular culture. Readers of the Disney comics were introduced at an early age to the money-obsessed Scrooge McDuck, Donald Duck's uncle. Apart from making even more money, much of Uncle Scrooge's time – awake as well as asleep –

appears to be spent worrying about the safety of his money and thwarting attempts, real or imagined, to steal it. Everyone, from close relatives to the notorious Beagle Boys (perhaps a metaphor for the proletariat) was out to get their hands on it.

More bitingly satirical is the figure of Mr Burns (Charles Montgomery Burns) from *The Simpsons* television animated cartoon series. The owner of the Springfield Nuclear Plant, a briber of federal officials and buyer of local judges, a backroom political kingmaker, a war profiteer, a Yale alumnus, Burns is a modern-day robber baron, 'the sneering face of capitalism'.

He is big business made wizened, liver-spotted flesh, the embodiment of the corporate world's black, rapacious heart. He *is* capital: ruthless, unfeeling, greedy, invincible … At the push of a button, Mr Burns can plunge Springfield into darkness or summon a squadron of oily-hided lawyers to annihilate his opponents. With a wave of his withered arm, he can bend the board of directors of Springfield University or the brains trust of the Republican Party to his will. He can buy his way out of a laundry list of environmental violations with the petty cash in his wallet, and then make an impulse purchase of the court's statue of Justice as an afterthought.[53]

As author Chris Turner notes in his study of the series, *Planet Simpson*, Mr Burns is not just ruthless in business but 'utterly rotten in all facets of his life'. He is disgusted by the concerns of ordinary people, not just thinking but *knowing* that he is a superior breed of human being. At the beginning of his trial for running over Bart Simpson in his car, his lawyer tells the judge; 'Your honour, my client has instructed me to remind the court how rich and important he is, that he is *not* like other men.' Then Mr Burns rises in court and barks: 'I should be able to run over as many kids as I want!'[54]

Echoes of Mr Burns and Uncle Scrooge are to be clearly heard in the words of Donald Trump whenever the conversation turns to his favourite topic – money, and the entitlement it brings. Clearly, his own sense of identity is defined by how much money has. In 2015, when he was starting his for the Republican nomination, Trump declared: 'I have total net worth of $8.73b. I'm not doing that to brag. I'm doing that to show that's the kind of thinking our country needs.' He took umbrage at a suggestion that he was not as rich as her claimed to be. In 2009, a judge dismissed a defamation suit Trump brought against Timothy O'Brien, author of *Trump Nation: The Art of Being the Donald*. O'Brien estimated Trump's wealth at $150m to $250m. Trump's estimate at the time the book was published was $5bn. [55]

In the run-up to the Iowa Republican caucuses in 2015, Trump boasted about his credentials, telling the *Des Moines Register* in an interview: 'I'm the most successful person ever to run for the presidency, by far. Nobody's ever been more successful than me. I'm the most successful person ever to run. Ross Perot isn't successful like me. Romney — I have a Gucci store that's worth more than Romney.'[56]

Two things rile Trump when it comes to matters of money. One, as we saw above, is any suggestion that his wealth claims are exaggerated; two is any idea he gets that someone is after, or has their hands on, his money. Nothing illustrates this more graphically, in almost comic cartoon style, than Trump's explosion when he learned that that former New Jersey governor, Chris Christie, who was at the time heading his transition team, was raising money for the operation. Summoning Christie and strategist Steve Bannon to Trump Tower, Trump was livid.

'Where the fuck is the money?' Trump asked Christie. 'I need money for my campaign. I'm putting money in my campaign, and you're fucking stealing from me.' He saw it all as his.[57]

Money was not just part of Trump's identity, it was central to it. An oft-repeated mantra was: 'Part of the beauty of me is that I am very rich.' Another was: 'You have to be wealthy in order to be great.'[58]

American success story

A curious reader of the future will take a book from the shelf, noting that the purported author was the 45th president of the United States. The book is called *Crippled America: How to Make America Great Again*, published in 2015 as Trump was beginning his run for the presidency. It was, like all books attributed to him, ghost written, but in this case unacknowledged.[59] Flicking through the pages, he or she will turn to the section 'About the Author', hoping to learn more about the man whose name appears on the title page. The section begins:

> Donald J. Trump is the very definition of the American success story, continually setting the standards of excellence while expanding his interests in real estate, sports, and entertainment. He is the archetypal businessman – a deal-maker without peer. [60]

Then follows thirteen pages, bristling with superlatives, in the same laudatory style. Then she is confronted by a list of dot points, compiled under the heading, 'Some of the properties owned and/or developed and managed or licensed by Donald J. Trump and the Trump Organization.' Starting with Trump Tower, Trump World Tower, and Trump Parc, through Trump Tower, Mumbai, India, and Trump Towers Istanbul, to Trump International Golf Club, Dubai, it is simply a catalogue of some eighty entries of businesses and residential real estate bearing the Trump name or association. It finishes with 'Corporate Aircrafts owned by Donald J. Trump', listing a Boeing 757, Cessna Citation X, and 3 Sikorsky 76 Helicopters.

What does this tell the curious reader? It says here is a man who is defined – and likes to be defined – by his wealth and possessions. Not intellectual achievement, cultural contribution, or public service, but by how much money he has (or says he has). Just in case you might miss the clues he throws out, they are everywhere – like Coca-Cola and McDonald's – and they all have his name on them, written large – TRUMP. They are right in your face; they are brash and gaudy; they are Trump personified. *The Economist* got it right when it described him as 'a man whose hobby is naming things after himself'.[61]

The Trump brand was everywhere; not just on real estate but also on hotel rooms, furniture, neckties, meat; almost anything that might be seen as high quality, high cost, high class. The kind of class Trump sought to deliver was 'defined not by social standing but by cash'. It was all aimed at the people who knew him from television.[62] He was selling the American Dream as personified by Donald Trump. He was the ultimate self-advertisement.

The Ugly American abroad

The world quickly began to notice about Donald Trump what many Americans already knew: he was boorish.

Just months into his presidency there he was on show before the world's cameras at the NATO summit meeting in Brussels. Trump had been critical of NATO, and other leaders were anxious about what he might say. But while his words had their expected controversy, just as much as what he did not say, it was something else that captured global attention: what the *Washington Post* called 'the fleeting, at best awkward interaction' between President Trump, the leader of the most powerful nation on Earth, and Dusko Markovic, the leader of Montenegro, a small Balkan nation of 600,000 attending its first summit as a NATO member after a nine-year accession process.

It occurred as NATO leaders strolled toward the place set up for a group photo. Trump reaches out his right arm, grabs Markovic's right shoulder and pushes him aside. Markovic looks surprised. Trump doesn't even acknowledge his existence as he moves past him. It's as if Markovic isn't there.

According to the *Post*, a slow-motion viewing of the video indicates no words spoken by Trump as he approaches the group from behind. No 'Excuse me' or 'Pardon me'. Markovic abruptly looks back at Trump but gets no eye contact from Trump in return. Then he pats Trump on the back, or perhaps the arm, displaying a slight grin as Trump, at the front of the group, stands tall and adjusts his suit coat. Trump begins conversing with Lithuanian President Dalia Grybauskaite as Markovic looks on from behind.

Reaction, especially in Montenegro, was immediate. Some news outlets included headlines quoting *Harry Potter* author J.K. Rowling, who tweeted the video saying 'You tiny, tiny, tiny little man' along with a retweeted video depicting Trump as a small man. One Montenegrin radio station posted on its website a photo of Trump above the story with the words 'Days without being a national embarrassment: 0.' 'It seems Donald Trump did not want anyone overshadowing his presence at the summit', said the Montenegro newspaper *Vijesti*. Other Balkan websites ran headlines such as 'America First' and 'Where do you think you are going?'[63]

The Ugly American was on full view.

4.

Contextualising Donald Trump: An Exceptional American or an American Exception?

The question: To what extent, if any, was Donald Trump an aberration, or was he an entirely predictable outcome of American circumstances?

The Celebrity

The future historian needs to be reminded that American voters in 2016 did not elect a politician as president; they elected a celebrity. What is a celebrity? It is, as an anonymous wit once defined it, someone who is famous for being famous. And that precisely was what Donald Trump was. Yet, was this really such a radical departure? In terms of Trump's immediate predecessors, it appeared so at first glance: he came after the policy-focused senator Barrack Obama; the former governor and scion of a political clan, George W. Bush; former governor Bill Clinton; political blueblood George H. W. Bush; actor but also former governor, Ronald Reagan;

former governor Jimmy Carter; long-serving congressman Gerald Ford; former vice-president Richard Nixon; and former senator John F. Kennedy. Trump, in contrast, had held no public office – yet he was widely known for being, well, widely known. It is possible to discern, though, certain trends at work that helped propel Trump into the White House, trends that had been long evident to astute observers.

In 1985, the social critic Neil Postman published his ground-breaking *Amusing Ourselves to Death: Public Discourse in the Age of Show Business* in which he explained how electronic media, especially television, were radically reshaping American culture and blurring the borders between entertainment and information. Postman argued that the fundamental metaphor for political discourse in America had become the television commercial, with its main aim to please the crowd and its principal instrument, artifice.[64]

More than two decades earlier, historian Daniel Boorstin, in his 1962 book, *The Image: A Guide to Pseudo Events in America*, had argued that political leaders were beginning to resemble 'media stars', rather than politicians, a development that was being aided and abetted by the news media. Boorstin further warned that if the voting public continued to be inundated with pseudo-events and un-nuanced media coverage, these media stars would soon dominate the political landscape.[65]

Donald Trump and American Exceptionalism

The United States does not consider itself to be like other nations. Indeed, from its Puritan origins to the present day, it has continued to bask in the wide-ranging (but also highly contested) notion of American Exceptionalism. There is little doubt that the notion in its various iterations has strongly shaped American culture, the way Americans see themselves and, perhaps more importantly, the way in which they see the world and their place and role in it. As cultural historian Deborah Madsen has noted, American exceptionalism 'permeates every period of American history and it is the single most powerful agent in a series of arguments that have been fought down the centuries concerning the identity of America and Americans.'[66]

There is, and has always been, a quasi-religious dimension to the notion of exceptionalism with many Americans believing America was chosen by Divine Providence to play a unique role in the shaping of history, not just in their own land but everywhere. For the early Puritans, fleeing religious persecution in Europe, America constituted the shining city on the hill; for Abraham Lincoln, it was the best hope of the human race; for Woodrow Wilson, involved in the remaking of the word order after World War I, America offered a model of how a free and democratic society could work in practice. The other nations of the world had only to copy what they saw to become similarly free and democratic.[67] Implicit in this is the idea the United States' history and mission endow it with a natural superiority over other nations.

The notion, as historian Margaret MacMillan wrote in relation to Wilson's efforts to create a League of Nations, has always had two sides to it:

> ... the one eager to set the world to rights, the other ready to turn its back with contempt if its

message should be ignored...Faith in their own exceptionalism has sometimes led to a certain obtuseness on the part of Americans, a tendency to preach at other nations rather than listen to them, a tendency as well to assume that American motives are pure where those of others are not ... [68]

Exceptionalism was not just a home-grown American conceit. The first reference to the concept by name, and possibly its origin, was by a perceptive outsider, the French writer Alexis de Tocqueville, in his seminal study published between 1835 and 1840, *Democracy in America*. He wrote that the position of the Americans is 'quite exceptional', noting in particular the universal prevalence of materialist concerns.

In America each man finds opportunities unknown elsewhere for making or for increasing his fortune. Greed is always in a breathless hurry; the human mind, constantly diverted from the pleasures of imaginative thought and labors of the intellect, is swayed only by the pursuit of wealth.[69]

It is not difficult to see the image of Donald Trump portrayed in these words from so long ago.

The idea of American exceptionalism weaves together multiple strands of meaning and interpretation, at times contradictory. At its base is an underlying belief that the history of the United States is inherently different from that of other nations in both its origins and trajectory.[70] In this view, American exceptionalism stems from its emergence from the American Revolution, thereby becoming what political scientist Seymour Martin Lipset called 'the first new nation'.[71]

Curiously, in an apparent contradiction of

Tocqueville, it has been claimed that America, rare among nations, was founded by intellectuals. As Richard Hofstadter wrote in his influential *Anti-Intellectualism in American Life* (1964): 'The Founding Fathers were sages, scientists, men of broad cultivation, many of them apt in classical learning, who used their wide reading in history, politics, and law to solve the exigent problems of the time.'[72] Yet, this enlightened state of affairs did not last. Casting a critical eye over the ravages to American society wrought by the hysteria of McCarthyism in the 1950s, Hofstadter goes on to ask how has it been possible, for much of the country's history since then, that the intellectual has been, for the most part, either an outsider, a servant, or a scapegoat.

'*A weird and improbable mixture*'

To be sure, the early settlers enjoyed an exceptional degree of personal liberty – and in that historical experience may be found the roots of an enduring strain of American libertarianism. Yet, the seedbed of that liberty was a product of unique historical, geographical, and cultural circumstances that were peculiar to that time and place. America started out, as one writer noted,

> as a weird and improbable mixture of an economy made up of self-sufficient farmers and small merchants, the Anglo-Saxon tradition of local government, the European peasant's tradition of hard work, the Calvinist tradition of the self-governing congregation, the Lutheran tradition of priesthood of every man, the absence of feudal institutions, the expanse and freshness of a colossal continent located in a new world.[73]

The product of these circumstances was a natural inclination towards libertarianism, and the wise Founding Fathers did not so much choose a strictly limited government for their new nation as simply recognise that this was the only form of government that would be tolerated by these people, instinctively resentful of any manner of interference in their own affairs by outsiders. It has been a source of tension and a political fault line ever since: from the anti-federalists, through to the whiskey rebellion of 1794, the civil war, and simmering resistance to government action as in the anti-trust laws enacted by Teddy Roosevelt, the New Deal of FDR, intervention in World War II, the Great Society program of LBJ and the modest health care proposals of Barack Obama.

Building on the back of the burgeoning Tea Party insurgency within the Republican Party – where that long-simmering resistance came to the fore – Donald Trump managed to tap into this vein by promising to 'drain the swamp' and Make America Great Again – an almost mystical reimagining of an elusive, but still powerful American Dream that, for many, had either vanished or never existed. Trump sought to project himself as the embodiment of that shimmering mirage.

In one view, Trumpism can be seen as part of a long continuing tradition and historical process rather than a rupture with the past. Donald Trump's presidency did not come out of the blue, according to political scientist, Peter J. Katzenstein, of Cornell University. His ideological inclinations can be neatly slotted into the history of American democracy. It is held up by the pillars of nationalism, evangelical Christianity, and an emphasis on ethnic identity, each of which is deeply rooted in the traditions and history of the United States.[74]

But in another view, argued by the distinguished international relations expert Joseph Nye, Jr., Trump can be seen as repudiating those aspects of American exceptionalism that inspired liberal internationalist efforts for both a world made freer and more peaceful through a system of international law and also for organisations that protect domestic liberty by moderating external threats.[75] In his study of the fourteen U.S. Presidents since World War II,[76] Nye wrote that Americans often see their country as exceptional because 'we define our identity not by ethnicity, but rather by ideas about a liberal vision of a society and way of life based on political, economic and cultural freedom. President Donald Trump's administration has departed from that tradition.'

Unlike his predecessors, Trump, for his part, rejected the very idea of American exceptionalism, even though the Republican Party as recently as 2013 had adopted it as a plank in its platform, defining it as 'the notion that our ideas and principles as a nation give us a unique place of moral leadership.' In late April 2015, a month before officially announcing his candidacy, he spoke at an event called 'Celebrating the American Dream' that was hosted in Houston by the Texas Patriots PAC, a local Tea Party outfit. Trump was asked to define American exceptionalism: 'Does American exceptionalism still exist? And what do we do to grow American exceptionalism?' In a rambling, barely coherent, reply, he admitted he did not like the term. 'I'll be honest with you. People say, "Oh he's not patriotic." Look, if I'm a Russian, or I'm a German, or I'm a person we do business with, why, you know, I don't think it's a very nice term. We're exceptional; you're not.'

But he left it open, adding: 'We may have a chance

to say it in the not-too-distant future. But even then, I wouldn't say it because when I take back the jobs, and when I take back all that money [from other countries] and we get all our stuff, I'm not going to rub it in. Let's not rub it in. Let's not rub it in. But I never liked that term.' The audience was silent.[77]

He seemed to imply from this that if he were to be elected – and only if he were elected -- America might just become exceptional.

It was not about America; it was about Donald Trump.

Donald Trump and the American Dream

The idea of the American Dream as some sort of shared national ethos is deeply embedded in American culture despite its disparate interpretations and contestations. Although the notion had been around for some time, inextricably linked to the broader concept of American Exceptionalism, the term itself was first used by historian James Truslow Adams in his 1931 book *The Epic of America*.

> The American dream is one of a land in which life should be better and richer and fuller for everyone, with opportunity for each according to ability or achievement. It is a difficult dream for the European upper classes to interpret adequately, and too many of us ourselves have grown weary and mistrustful of it. It is not a dream of motor cars and high wages merely, but a of social order in which each man and each woman shall be able to attain to the fullest stature of which they are innately capable, and be recognized by others for what they are, regardless of the fortuitous circumstances of birth or position.[78]

In 2007, *Forbes* interviewed a New York real estate developer and television show host, Donald J. Trump, who offered his own thoughts on the American Dream.

The American Dream is freedom, prosperity, peace--and liberty and justice for all. That's a big dream. It's not always easy to achieve, but that's the ideal. More than any country in history we've made gains toward a democracy that is enviable throughout the world. Dreams require perseverance if they are to be realized, and fortunately we're a hard-working country and people. We are the luckiest people in history, just by the fact that we are Americans.[79]

Yet, less than a decade after speaking these words, the same Donald Trump – by this time a contender for the Republican presidential nomination – again invoked the American Dream, but only to pronounce it dead. In June 2015, from a podium inside Trump Tower in Manhattan, Donald Trump kicked off his presidential campaign with the announcement: 'This country is a hellhole. We are going down fast. We can't do anything right. We're a laughingstock all over the world. The American dream is dead.'[80] Only he could restore it; he alone could breathe life back into that corpse; he would save America and revive the American Dream.

Of course, invoking the American Dream as a political ploy was no novelty; all presidents since the Adams book appeared had done so, employing its powerful symbolism to serve a variety of causes as a catalyst for action. These included: *tenant farmers* (FDR), *a better life for the next generation* (Truman), *medical care and hospitals* (Eisenhower), *space exploration* (Kennedy), *civil rights* (Johnson), *college education* (Nixon), *home ownership* (Ford), *environmental protection* (Carter), *a beacon of freedom* (Reagan), *immigration reform* (George H. W. Bush and George W. Bush), *small businesses* (Clinton) and *jobs* (Obama).

But not Donald Trump; this time it was different. One commentary went so far as to accuse Trump of mounting a coup against the key tenet of American idealism by 'weaponizing it to convince Americans that the pursuit of life, liberty and happiness can only be revived by a single man.' That is what Trump effectively did in declaring his candidacy for president, and that is exactly what he continued to do as president, doubling down on 'the deeply cynical lie that America's greatness is contingent upon his grip on power – that the institutions meant to protect our liberty and prosperity are disposable.'[81]

Within Trump's inner circle, an oft-repeated mantra was that the American people had elected him to revive the American Dream. His sycophantic vice-president, Mike Pence, said in an interview in 2019 that the dream was dying until Trump's inauguration in 2017. He said that before Trump became president, trade deals pushed car manufacturers out of the country, but Trump fought 'for trade deals that put American jobs and American workers first'.

> I really do believe that's why the American people chose a president whose family lived the American dream and was willing to go in and fight to make the American dream available for every American.[82]

There is little doubt that for many Americans, the idea of the dream had soured. Indeed, for many, including the majority of African-Americans, it was never really entertained as a possibility at all.

Cultural critic Chris Hedges wrote in 2012 that the 'American dream, we now know, is a lie'.

> The vaunted American dream, the idea that life will get better, that progress is inevitable if we obey the rules and work hard, that material prosperity is assured, has been replaced by a hard and bitter truth ... We will all be sacrificed. The virus of corporate abuse – the perverted belief that only corporate profit matters – has spread to outsource our jobs, cut the budgets of our schools, close our libraries, and plague our communities with foreclosures and unemployment.[83]

Even as Trump struggled with his self-appointed mission to resurrect the American Dream, the American people themselves remained sceptical. An opinion poll by RealClearPolitics conducted in February 2019 offered a snapshot on the state of the Dream under Donald Trump.

- 37% of the poll's voters said the American Dream was still alive – but under threat;
- 28% said it was under serious threat – but there was still hope;
- 7% said it was dead; and
- 27% said it was alive and well.[84]

Interestingly, just over half of the respondents (51%) felt that President Trump had made it more difficult to attain the American Dream while 30% believed he had made it easier.

The Dream as metaphor

At its core, the American Dream is a metaphor for an all-American mentality, an aspiration as well as an idealised shared ethos. Essentially, it is a version of a rags-to-riches story, a log-cabin-to-White House journey, neither of which, on even a cursory glance, apply even remotely to Donald J. Trump – born into wealth and privilege, launched into business through his father's fortune, and using it to buy celebrity status. Yet Donald Trump continued to present himself as the living embodiment of this imagined land of milk and honey, promising to resurrect the American Dream for all.

As *U.S. Business News* noted in a commentary, Trump's own policies reflected a very selective interpretation (or even a distortion) of the American Dream – a dream only for the few, not the many (and, indeed, at the expense of the many). In an attempt to stimulate economic growth, Trump altered the tax landscape in America by cutting taxes for corporations and small businesses, which further enriched the wealthiest while not helping the average person. 'Tax relief for the rich to middle classes highlights the rising financial inequality that the American Dream is trying to dispel', it noted.

> Looking at the American population, a huge percentage of Americans lack exactly that starting point, which would give them access to the American Dream advocated by their president. Donald Trump's story has somehow altered the original idea of the American Dream, meaning some groups are put into a privileged position and have more chances to living the American Dream.[85]

Cynically, Trump well understood that while many Americans suspected that the economic game was rigged to favour the rich, they still wanted to be rich themselves. One perceptive biographer, writing before Trump became president, noted how Trump quite deliberately played on the idea in his relentless self-promotion.

> His rise to prominence in 1978 coincided, almost exactly, with the moment when median wages stopped growing and the earnings of those in the highest ranks took off. At that same time the mass media became swollen with lifestyle and celebrity 'news', a kind of pornography of wealth and fame. As the public feasted on images of excess, Trump's face was associated with all the tantalizing pleasures that many could buy. Obscured by hype, the facts of his life didn't matter as much as the idea of him.[86]

Had the idea of Donald Trump supplanted the American Dream? Had Trump appropriated the American Dream just as he had the notion of American exceptionalism?

5.

Historical Comparisons

Men of his kind behave the same way in private life,
before they have gained power – Plato

The historian of the future might be tempted, on the evidence, to see Donald Trump as *sui generis*. But casting an eye back in time it would be possible, for all Trump's apparent singularity, to discern in both his character and *modus operandi* certain shared traits and characteristics with other historical figures.

What sort of ruler was he? Certainly, he exhibited clear authoritarian tendencies; he was erratic, unpredictable, wilful; he was cruel and he liked to humiliate both friend and foe; he was undoubtedly a populist, shamelessly appealing to the masses to oppose certain elites, in his case the despised 'political class', the self-serving denizens of the Washington swamp that had to be drained. And it would be noted that the contemporaries with whom he had the greatest rapport were not democrats but ruthless authoritarians like Putin in Russia and Erdogan in Turkey. But was he a tyrant?

Turning to the great Aristotle – who first classified political types of rulers – it might be noted that Donald Trump is captured, if only partially, in

Aristotle's definition: 'Tyranny is a kind of monarchy which has in view the interest of the monarch only.'[87] Trump, of course, was not a monarch, but he exercised political power largely for his own benefit rather than public good: self-enrichment was always his top priority.

In his consideration of the question of tyranny, which was rife in Aristotle's time, the philosopher discerned three basic types. In the first type, a usurper gains and keeps power by force – which, of course, is not Trump. In the second type, Aristotle identified 'elected monarchs who exercise a despotic power' – that is closer. Aristotle's third kind of tyranny, 'the most typical form', is more difficult: it applies and does not apply in equal measure. Aristotle notes that this kind of tyranny 'is just that arbitrary power of an individual which is responsible to no one, and governs all alike … with a view to its own advantage, not to that of its subjects, and therefore against their will.'

Plato also turned his attention to the question of tyranny and the character of the tyrant. A tyrant, for Plato, wasn't just someone who ruled over others; a tyrant is someone who can't rule over himself. He's Eros incarnate – pure impulse, always in the thrall of his own lusts and passions.[88] Plato likens the tyrant to a drunken man, in whom there is a constant 'succession of passions, and the new gets the better of the old and takes away their rights'. Because he can't get along without domineering or being served, moreover, he 'never tastes of true freedom or friendship'. Tellingly, Plato writes of the similarities in private life and public life.

Men of his kind behave the same way in private life, before they have gained power. Their companions are subservient parasites, and they are themselves always prepared to give way and put on the most extravagant act of friendship if it suits their purpose, though once that purpose is achieved their tune changes.[89]

Cleon

From ancient Greece, it is hard not to see close parallels with the ruthless Athenian politician Cleon from the fifth century BCE. Just like Donald Trump, he inherited a business from his father and became the first leader drawn from the commercial classes. Part populist and part plutocrat, Cleon sought support from the lower orders by promising all sorts of rewards and for a time he was in alliance with other wealthy sections of society (although he later broke with them). Various accounts depict Cleon as rough and unpolished, although he was said to have a natural eloquence and a powerful voice and knew exactly how to work upon the feelings of the people. There were those in Athens at the time who warned of the dangers ahead under Cleon's leadership.[90] Just as Trump loathed the political class, so, too, did Cleon despise the political class of his day, the nobility.

As one astute scholar has observed, Cleon also used the Peloponnesian War (Athens's great war with Sparta) to garner popular support. The great historian of that war, Thucydides, was highly critical of Cleon, observing that he was 'remarkable among the Athenians for the violence of his character'. By ranging Athenians against an enemy, he could unite them behind himself just as Trump used apocalyptic and deeply misleading rhetoric about crime, immigrants, Muslims, and the economy to create a climate of existential fear in which he presented himself as the sole source of salvation.[91]

The similarity did not end there. Cleon and Trump shared the same weakness: a thin-skinned inability to endure ridicule. Aristophanes wrote plays mercilessly mocking Cleon, which drove him into a rage, even to the extent of suing the playwright. Trump reacted similarly to *Saturday Night Live's* portrayal of him. He also, like Cleon, sued a comedian who mocked him: Bill Maher.[92]

David Clifton, writing in *The Harvard Crimson*, noted how both Cleon and Trump shared a blatant disregard for the norms which form the bedrock of the democratic process, Clifton quoting Plutarch: 'Cleon stripped the bema of its decorum, setting the fashion of yelling when he harangued the people... He thus imbued the managers of the city's policies with that levity and contempt for propriety which soon after confounded the whole state.' Clifton continues:

Trump's mockery of a disabled reporter, his condescending midnight tweets, his disparagement of critics and the media, his casual incitements to violence at rallies, his lewd remarks about women, his attacks on federal judges, his unending boasting and unparalleled hyperbole, his pathological mendacity, and even his tendency to speak in rambling or incomplete sentences all subvert the basic standards of civil discourse necessary for the healthy functioning of a democratic society. He has stripped the American bema of its decorum, and the nation risks being confounded.

Further, Cleon pursued a damaging 'Athens First' policy, anticipating Trump's 'America First' platform, prolonging the Peloponnesian War in the hopes of Athenian domination, and through his example replacing bluster with wisdom in the deliberations of the Assembly, enabling additional power-hungry demagogues to rise to prominence and sustain Athens's decline after his death.[93] He died in battle in 422 BCE.

Caligula

In a later era, the comparison with the Roman Empire's Caligula (formally Gaius Julius Caesar Augustus Germanicus) from the first century is irresistible. The third Roman emperor began his term seemingly popular with the common people but with many sceptics among the educated classes. Accounts of his later rule highlight his cruelty, sadism, harsh treatment of officials, extravagance, and sexual proclivities, presenting him as an insane tyrant, bent on inexhaustible self-aggrandisement.

During his brief reign of almost four years, Caligula worked assiduously to dismantle any vestiges of accountability, increasing the unconstrained personal power of the emperor. He liked to champion big construction projects and especially liked his name emblazoned on monuments, such as two aqueducts in Rome, the Aqua Claudia and the Anio Novus.

To gain support at the start of his term, he granted bonuses to the military, including the city troops and the army outside Italy, not to mention significant tax cuts for many. Ignoring economic advice from officials, Caligula's erratic management of finances led to a brief famine, attributed by the historian, Seneca, to the severe disruption of grain imports because Caligula re-purposed grain boats for a pontoon bridge built in his honour, linking the resort of Baiae to the neighbouring port of Puteoli. Contemporary accounts speculate that the bridge was to rival the Persian king Xerxes's pontoon bridge crossing of the Hellespont.

Caligula, who could not swim, then proceeded to ride his favourite horse, Incitatus, across, wearing the breastplate of Alexander the Great. This act was in defiance of a prediction by Tiberius's soothsayer, Thrasyllus of Mendes, that Caligula had 'no more chance of becoming emperor than of riding a horse across the Bay of Baiae'.[94]

While there is no evidence that he ever actually appointed his horse to the Senate, he certainly alluded to the prospect as a mark of his contempt for the worthies who sat there. His end was grisly: he was assassinated.

Like Donald Trump, Caligula was a self-proclaimed genius, and would inflict cruel and arbitrary punishments upon those who failed to acknowledge his genius and flatter him. His cruelty was matched by his savage language along with a hatred of anyone or anything that stood in his way, telling his own grandmother, who sought to chide him: 'Bear in mind that I can do anything I want to anyone I want!'[95] He even threatened to abolish the study of law, swearing that no legal expert's advice would ever thwart his will.[96] (Compare this with Trump's systematic removal of oversighting officials in the administration.)

To survive in Caligula's inner circle, it was quickly realised, you had to flatter the leader. Similarly, those around Trump abased themselves outrageously to remain in his favour. The flattery can seem over the top. For example, White House aide Stephen Miller went on television and called Trump a 'political genius'. In an early Cabinet meeting, Vice President Mike Pence praised Trump so effusively that it prompted widespread mockery and comparisons to authoritarian cults of personality. And it did not end there. In June 2017, commentators were similarly startled after members of the Cabinet took turns praising him in barely believable terms.[97]

Also like Donald Trump, Caligula's predatory sexuality was mixed with a sadistic urge to humiliate the partners and husbands of those on whom he preyed. Suetonius describes how Caligula would invite a selection of couples to dinner, slowly and carefully examining each woman in turn while they passed his couch, 'as a purchaser might assess the value of a slave', occasionally stretching out his hand and lifting up the chin of any who kept her eyes modestly cast down. Then, whenever he felt so inclined, he would send for whoever pleased him best and leave the banquet in her company. A little later he would return, showing obvious signs of what he had been about, and openly discuss his bedfellow in detail, dwelling on her good and bad physical points and criticizing her sexual performance. To some of these unfortunates he issued, and publicly registered, divorces in the name of their absent husbands.[98]

Compare this with an account of Trump's about his boast that one of the things that made life worth living was getting your friends' wives into bed. According to Michael Wolff, in *Fire and Fury*, Trump, in pursuing a friend's wife, would try to persuade the wife that her husband was perhaps not what she thought.

> Then he'd have his secretary ask the friend into his office; once the friend arrived, Trump would

engage in what was, for him, more or less constant sexual banter. *Do you still like having sex with your wife? How often? You must have had a better fuck than your wife? Tell me about it. I have girls coming in from Los Angeles at three o'clock, We can go upstairs and have a great time, I promise ...* And all the while, Trump would have his friend's wife on the speakerphone, listening in.[99]

Caligula at some point in his erratic reign began to think of himself as god. When several client kings came to Rome to pay their respects to him and argued about their nobility of descent, he allegedly cried out the Homeric line: 'Let there be one lord, one king.' His audience was left in no doubt as to the identity of the great one. Caligula began insisting on being treated as a god, and arranged for some famous statues, such as those of Jupiter, to be brought from Greece to have their heads replaced with his own likeness.[100] In the year 40, Caligula began implementing controversial policies that introduced religion into his hitherto secular political role, and took to appearing in public dressed as various gods and demigods. According to Cassius Dio's account, he began referring to himself as a god when meeting with politicians and he was referred to as 'Jupiter' on occasion in public documents. Caligula took things a step further and had those in Rome, including senators, worship him as a tangible, living god.[101]

Though not outwardly religious, Donald Trump did not shy away from Messiah-like allusions; indeed, he even brazenly referred to himself as 'the chosen one'. The context was a media conference in 2019 about, of all things, growing tensions over trade between the United States and China during which Trump said revamping the countries' trade relationship should have been done 'a long time ago by a lot of other presidents'. He then opened his arms, looked toward the sky and said: 'I am the chosen one. Somebody had to do it, so I'm taking on China ... and you know what we're winning.'[102]

It might have been dismissed as a tongue-in-cheek throwaway line – and certainly the journalists present laughed – but it fed into a narrative that was already running, and eagerly taken up by the Christian right-wing in the U.S. Earlier in 2019, former White House press secretary, Sarah Huckabee Sanders, told the Christian Broadcasting Network that the president was called by God. She said: 'I think God calls all of us to fill different roles at different times and I think that He wanted Donald Trump to become president.'[103] Another Trump insider, Energy Secretary Rick Perry, said in an interview that he had told the president that he was God's 'chosen one' to lead the United States, just as God had chosen the kings to lead Israel in the Old Testament.[104]

A long-time observer of Trump, CNN political analyst, Chris Cillizza,[105] was among those who cautioned against writing off Trump's 'chosen one' remark as a joke; indeed, he argued, it constituted a central part of Trump's own belief system. Two serious strains of Trump thought were at work in the 'chosen one' moment: one was his oft-repeated claim to be special and unique. ('I alone can fix it', he boasted during his campaign after listing America's problems); the other was his addiction to exaggeration and theatrics. Trump himself drew attention to this facet of his behaviour in his 1987 book, *Trump: The Art of the Deal*.

The final key to the way I promote is bravado. I play

70

to people's fantasies. People may not always think big themselves, but they can get very excited by those who do. That is why a little hyperbole never hurts. People want to believe that something is the biggest, the greatest and the most spectacular.[106]

Just as Caligula began to introduce religious themes into his rule, so, too, did Trump. In June 2020, as protests continued around the country over yet another police killing of an unarmed African-American, Trump had security forces use tear gas and batons to clear a path for him through a crowd of peaceful protestors outside the White House in order for him to pose for a picture while holding a bible and standing outside a church, which had been damaged by fire the previous night. Trump did not enter the church.[107] According to the *New York Times*, Trump 'made no pretense of any intent other than posing for photographs – he held up the Bible carried by his daughter, then gathered a few top advisers next to him in a line.'[108]

The similarities do not end there. Donald Trump has never concealed his quick eye for making a dollar. This continued into his presidency, according to a citizens' watchdog organisation, Citizens for Responsibility in Ethics in Washington. In a report in 2019, it said Trump's failure to divest from his businesses and his actions as president had resulted in more than 2,300 conflicts in just three years of interest between his administration and his personal financial interests, notably the constant advertising and official patronage of his businesses.[109] Of Caligula, Suetonius writes:

He never missed a chance of making profits: setting aside a suite of rooms on the Palatine, he decorated them worthily, opened a brothel, stocked it with married women and freeborn boys, and then sent his pages around the squares and public places, inviting men of all ages to come and enjoy themselves. Those who appeared were lent money at interest, and clerks wrote down their names under the heading 'Contributors to Caesar's Revenue'.[110]

Even in recreation, both Caligula and Trump liked to win at any cost, even through cheating. Suetonius wrote of how at dice, the emperor would 'always cheat and lie'.[111] The golf writer, Rick Reilly, says much the same about Trump at golf: 'Trump doesn't just cheat at golf ... He cheats like a three-card Monte dealer. He throws it, boots it, and moves it. He lies about his lies. He fudges and foozles and fluffs.'[112]

Mussolini

In more recent times, there are clear parallels with Donald Trump and the Italian Fascist leader Benito Mussolini, Italy's prime minister from 1922 until 1943 (although the Italian had read some books). Each paid careful attention to his public appearances, always meticulously stage-managed. Mussolini's comic pomposity in the rigid stance and thrusting jaw can easily be seen in Trump's very deliberate way of walking and holding himself stiffly in public. (A prescient 2005 episode of the animated television satire *The Simpsons* portrayed Homer Simpson, on a visit to Italy, speaking from a balcony, making extravagant gestures and striking exaggerated poses, which prompts Lisa to ask him 'not to imitate Mussolini'. Homer then says he was actually imitating Donald Trump.)[113]

An American history professor, Ruth Ben-Ghiat, author of several studies on Italian Fascism, has noted striking similarities between Trump and Mussolini, even down to the distinctive flourish of the signatures. Both portrayed themselves as outsiders, siding with 'the people' against the political establishment. In an interview with the *New Yorker*,[114] she noted how when Mussolini was a socialist, he wrote his name as 'Benito Mussolini', but then he dropped the Benito, even adopting a stylized stage name, 'Il Duce' (The Leader). Trump also likes talking about himself in the third person, either by name or simply as 'The Donald'. 'He's selling his product, which is himself', she said, adding that it was a cult of personality peddled as good business. 'They have this hunger for approval. But their personas are created by the symbiosis with the crowd. They need the crowd to consolidate their personalities.'

Ben-Ghiat described both men as essentially 'mass marketers. They pick up what's in the air.' The film reel was to Mussolini as Twitter is to Trump; each medium used in a way to create the impression of talking directly to the people. They can be portentous and relentlessly self-assertive. In a way, authoritarians have to be, Ben-Ghiat explained, since they're selling a paradox: a saviour fashioned as the truest, most authentic expression of the masses. She noted how Trump summed it up baldly at the Republican Convention that anointed him: 'I am your voice. I alone can fix it.' The authoritarian makes the contradiction fall away, like an optical illusion.

Writing in *The Atlantic*, Professor Ben-Ghiat observed that Italians learned in the 1920s what Americans were learning in 2016.

Charismatic authoritarians seeking political office

cannot be understood through the framework of traditional politics. They lack interest in, and patience for, established protocols. They often trust few outside of their own families, or those they already control, making collaboration and relationship building difficult. They work from a different playbook, and so must those who intend to confront them.[115]

Elaborating on the methods employed, Ben-Ghiat noted how Mussolini's rise to power also exemplifies another authoritarian trait America has seen during the 2016 presidential campaign: 'The charismatic leader who tests the limits of what the public, press, and political class will tolerate.' She wrote how this exploration begins early and is accomplished through highly controversial actions and the use of threatening or humiliating remarks directed at targeted groups or individuals. The purpose of such tactics was 'to gauge the collective appetite and permission for verbal and physical violence and the use of extra-legal methods in policing and other realms'. The way elites and the press respond to each example of boundary-pushing sets the tone for the leader's future behaviour – and that of his followers, she wrote.

The parallels with Mussolini are far from fleeting. Candidate Trump happily embraced key elements associated with the Italian, such as the maxim 'It is better to live one day as a lion than 100 years as a sheep', approvingly retweeted to his then 6.5 million followers in 2016.[116] Even his pledge to 'drain the swamp' – code for attacking the political establishment and dismantling the administrative state – derives from Mussolini's *drenare la palude*, according to former US Secretary of State, Madeleine Albright.[117] Mussolini declared his mission was to restore past (real or imagined) glories – not all that far removed from making America great again. Never one to shy away from violent rhetoric, he said that his mission was 'to break the bones of the democrats … and the sooner the better'.

Continuing her comparison, Albright highlights Mussolini's talent for theatre, and how he was a poor listener who disliked hearing other people talk. He discouraged cabinet members from 'proposing any idea that might cause him to doubt his instincts', which, he insisted, were always right. He also promoted the idea of national self-sufficiency 'without ever grasping how unrealistic that ambition had become'.

Comparisons with the Fascist dictator were not confined to Trump's political opponents; indeed, there were even those within the Republican Party who voiced such concerns, like Congressman Chris Stewart of Utah who, on 10 March 2016 before Trump had clinched the party's nomination, tweeted: 'Donald Trump does not represent Republican ideals, he is our Mussolini. Donald Trump's approach is – I am just going to do it.'[118] But, like many of his colleagues hitherto critical of Trump, Stewart fell meekly into line.

A decorated retired four-star general, Barry McCaffrey, saw a similarity with the Italian dictator when in late 2019 President Trump ordered the cancellation of all government subscriptions to the *New York Times* and *Washington Post*. In a much-publicised tweet, he wrote:

> The White House Trump statement telling the entire Federal Government to terminate subscriptions to the NYT and Wash Post is a watershed moment in national history. No room for HUMOROUS media

coverage. This is deadly serious. This is Mussolini.[119]

Other parallels

Donald Trump's populism has been compared with that of Argentina's Juan Perón; his demand for, and susceptibility to, flattery is like that of Romanian dictator, Nicolae Ceausescu. More subtly, his often indirect mode of communication, frequently taking the form of a code understood by his followers, exhibits similarities with the Spanish dictator, Francisco Franco.

It was said of Franco that he was 'a man who says things and unsays them, who draws near and slips away, he vanishes and trickles away; always vague and never clear or categoric'.[120] Trump similarly exhibited this elusive quality, such as his off-handed remark in a candidate debate in 2016 when he appeared to incite violence against his rival Hillary Clinton, saying elliptically: 'If she gets to pick her judges, nothing you can do, folks. Although the Second Amendment people, maybe there is. I don't know.'[121] The Second Amendment is about the right to bear arms.

Another example of this was at a rally in 2015 when he was campaigning for the Republican nomination. A woman told him: 'We have a problem in this country. It's called Muslims', and asked him: 'When can we get rid of them?' Trump replied: 'We're going to be looking at a lot of different things, and a lot of people are saying that, and a lot of people are saying that bad things are happening out there. We're going to be looking at that and plenty of other things.'[122]

Like Germany's Adolf Hitler, Trump could work

a crowd to perfection. While Hitler reached deep into the darker recesses of the national psyche with his crafted rhetoric, Trump's wellspring was reality television, replete with caustic putdowns, glib one-liners and inarticulate, unfinished sentences that invite the audience to complete. In each case, a version of the 'stab-in-the-back' theory is presented: in the former it was democracy, socialists and Jews; in the latter, the political establishment, the Democrats, China, and the UN (or any other target of the moment).

On another level, the Trump presidency carried echoes of the syphilitic sociopath, Idi Amin, who presided over Uganda from 1971 to 1979, whose despotic rule was accompanied by a constant projection of delusional fantasies. Ruling by decree after earlier promising elections, Amin's behaviour became increasingly bizarre and unpredictable. After the United Kingdom broke off diplomatic relations with his regime in 1977, Amin declared that he had defeated the British, and he conferred on himself the decoration, among others, of CBE (Conqueror of the British Empire). He also claimed to be uncrowned King of Scotland.

But at a more serious level, there were elements of Trump's rule that bore more than passing resemblance to the latter years of China's Mao Zedong. Sensing that power was slipping away from him, Mao unleashed the Cultural Revolution that convulsed the country for a decade from the mid-1960s, mobilising the masses against his perceived enemies in the political establishment. The historian of the Cultural Revolution, Frank Dikötter, wrote that Mao 'combined grandiose ideas about his own historical destiny with an extraordinary capacity for malice. He was easily offended and resentful, with a long memory for grievances.'[123]

While Trump's supporters were certainly not the brutal Red Guards of China, television images in mid-2020 of angry mobs, among them many carrying weapons, coming out to support the president's call for an end to lockdowns against the coronavirus pandemic, offered a chilling premonition of what might be ahead – especially if Trump lost an election he claimed was rigged. Some of the armed incursions even took place in state legislatures as law enforcement just stood by.

In late April, in Lansing, Michigan, members of the self-styled 'American Patriot Rally' stormed the state's capitol building, singing the national anthem and chanting 'Let us work.' It was the largest of several protests in the city after Trump supporters had earlier organised thousands of people for 'Operation Gridlock' which jammed the streets with cars to call out what they said was the overreach of Democratic Governor Gretchen Whitmer's strict stay-at-home order.

Trump applauded their actions, praising the occupiers and urging the governor to bend to their will. 'The Governor of Michigan should give a little and put out the fire. These are very good people', Trump tweeted, echoing his defence of the 'very fine people' demonstrating at a white nationalist rally in Charlottesville in 2017. 'But they are angry', Trump said of the Michigan protesters. 'They want their lives back again, safely! See them, talk to them, make a deal.'[124]

Trump appeared to take great political comfort from the chaos, just as Mao Zedong had done in China with the chaos he set in train; it was to both a political instrument. A saying oft attributed to Mao is: 'Everything under heaven is in utter chaos; the situation is excellent.' In a letter at the start of the Cultural Revolution, he wrote to his wife expressing his determination to create *'great disorder under heaven'* for the purpose of ultimately achieving *'great order under heaven'*.[125]

Early in 2016, when there was still significant opposition within the Republican Party to Donald Trump's nomination, even as he led the field of candidates in the primaries, Trump issued a stern warning about what might happen if he were deprived of the nomination because of falling just short of the number of delegates required. There could be 'problems like you've never seen before. I think bad things would happen' and 'I think you'd have riots'.[126]

In comments made on television in 2014, long before he entered the presidential race, Donald Trump told Fox News that 'total hell' would make America 'great' again. The then television was commenting on, among other things, the rate of unemployment. He said: 'You know what solves it? When the economy crashes, when the economy goes to total hell and everything is a disaster ... then you'll have, you know, you'll have riots to go back to where we were when we were great.'[127]

By late 2020, the economy was faltering due to the coronavirus restrictions, unemployment was soaring and sporadic rioting had broken out, spilling over from protests and counter-demonstrations about police violence against black Americans. Blaming violence on 'leftists' and 'anarchists', Trump declared himself 'your president of law and order'.[128] The implication was clear: only he could fix it.

Donald Trump had his chaos.

6.

The Historical Trump

*Actually, throughout my life, my two greatest assets
have been mental stability and being, like, really smart.*
– Donald J. Trump

Autobiography for a historian is useful – but it has
its limitations, and is always treated with caution,
if not outright scepticism. It is useful in that one
can check events and dates with other accounts but
the limitation comes with knowing it is, by its very
nature, self-serving, selective and, in many cases,
simply false. But knowing this, the historian reads
on, always curious to see what the subject sees when
he or she looks in the mirror.

Self-portrait

The future historian of the Trump era will face
a bewildering array of quotes attributed to the
president. Unlike previous studies of the past and
the challenge of matching colourful quote with
truth, little time will be spent pondering their
authenticity – especially as so many of them were
tweeted personally by the president. The inevitable
head-scratching will come not so much from
puzzlement but from amazement that they were
actually said at all.

Then there is the problem of context. How does one manage to connect dots when no connection seems possible? Take, for example, Trump's comment on gay marriage, quoted in the *New York Times* (1 May 2011), several years before he became president.

> It's like in golf ... A lot of people – I don't want this to sound trivial – but a lot of people are switching to these really long putters, very unattractive...it's weird. You see these great players with these really long putters, because they can't sink three-footers anymore. And, I hate it. I am a traditionalist. I have so many fabulous friends who happen to be gay, but I am a traditionalist.

Excuse me? Was this a question about golf or a social issue to which he was responding? But then his positions are never fixed – this self-proclaimed traditionalist in office would be anything but a traditionalist.

What emerges from the vast autobiographical archive of Donald Trump is that Donald Trump was the most remarkable man who ever lived. As he told his chief of staff, John Kelly, when Kelly proposed a briefing on a certain subject: 'I don't want to talk to anyone. I know more than they do. I know better than anybody else.'[129]

Those around him began to take note of his increasingly extravagant claims to expert knowledge, and among them were:

- On campaign finance: 'I think nobody knows more about campaign finance than I do, because I am the biggest contributor.'

- On the courts: 'I know more about courts than any human being on Earth.'

- On trade: 'Nobody knows more about trade than me.'

- On taxes: 'Nobody knows more about taxes than I do.'

- On ISIS: 'I know more about ISIS than the generals do.'

- On the U. S. government: 'Nobody knows the system better than I do.'

- On technology: 'Technology – nobody knows more about technology than me.'[130]

And what he often started out talking about was often not where he was going. For example, a rambling address to the Central Intelligence Agency in the first few days of his presidency, seemingly designed to ingratiate himself with the military and intelligence communities, veered into an absurd self-promotion.

> I know a lot about West Point, I'm a person who very strongly believes in academics. Every time I say I had an uncle who was a great professor at MIT for 35 years, who did a fantastic job in so many ways academically – and then they say, Is Donald Trump an intellectual? Trust me, I'm, like, a smart person.[131]

Self-promotion was a recurring theme, whether related to his intelligence, physical attributes, or achievements.

- To be blunt, people would vote for me. They just would. Why? Maybe because I'm so good looking. (*New York Times*, 19 September 1999).

- I'm intelligent. Some people would say I'm very, very, very intelligent. (*Fortune*, 3 April 2000).

- I look very much forward to showing my financials, because they are huge. (*Time*, 14 April 2011).

- … part of the beauty of me is that I am very rich. (ABC's 'Good Morning America', March 2011).

- My fingers are long and beautiful as, it has been well documented, are various other parts of my body. (*New York Post*, 2011).

- Sorry losers and haters, but my IQ is one of the highest – and you all know it! Please don't feel so stupid or insecure, it's not your fault. (Twitter, 9 May 2013).

- ... Actually, throughout my life, my two greatest assets have been mental stability and being, like, really smart. I went from VERY successful businessman to top TV star to President of the United States (on my first try). I think that would qualify as not smart, but genius … and a very stable genius at that! (Twitter, 6 January 2018).

A Twitter tyrant?

Given that Twitter is Trump's preferred medium of communication, it will fall to tomorrow's historian to sift through countless thousands of these. Many of them will make no sense at all, relating to an event or comment long forgotten; others will simply be puerile name-calling of opponents or hitting back at criticism; many will be self-congratulatory. Will they tell the historian anything useful? Possibly.

Using an analytical tool called Moral Foundations Theory (MFT),[132] political scientist Gregg R. Murray randomly selected 30 days of Trump's tweets between the day he announced his candidacy in 2015 until the end of May 2016, resulting in 290 tweets or almost 10 tweets per day.

Writing in *Psychology Today*, he found that Trump used a preponderance of words pertaining to authority, placing him in a category of MFT known as authority/subversion, one of five universal foundations it identifies (among care/harm, fairness/cheating, loyalty/betrayal, and sanctity/degradation). This foundation, according to the originators of the theory, was shaped by 'our long primate history of hierarchical social interactions. It underlies virtues of leadership and followership, including deference to legitimate authority and respect for traditions.' Words that reflect authority include *obey, duty, respect, authority, permission, command* and *comply*. On the other hand, words that indicate subversion include *defiance, disobey, lawless, protest, disrespect, unfaithful* and *obstruct*.

In the study sample, Trump was much more likely to use authority-based words in his tweets – in particular *control, honor, illegal, leader, refuse, respected* and *status* – than any of the other types of MFT-based words. He used words related to authority/subversion 9.5% of the time, which is nearly 50% more than his next most widely used category, fairness/cheating, which he used 6.4% of the time.

In comparison, a similar analysis of tweets by Hillary Clinton, his Democratic opponent for the presidency, shows Trump used authority-based words almost three times more often than she did. Clinton, on the other hand, was much more likely to use care-based words, such as compassion and hurt, locating her in the care/harm foundation that focuses on whether a person prevents or relieves harm to others.

Addressing the question of whether Trump's words suggest he is a tyrant, Murray hesitates to pass judgment 'given the extraordinarily negative connotations of the word', but he adds: 'To me it means he frequently thinks in terms of social hierarchies and accompanying norms.'[133]

Trump's political appeal

Looking back at the figure that emerges from contemporary accounts, we might be tempted to laugh at Donald Trump at our peril. The undisguised disdain of the political cognoscenti – seeing just a crude, uneducated and inarticulate figure – might well be directed at a caricature, not the real Trump who made it into the White House. The real Trump just might not have been so much a bumbling, wealthy fool who bought and lied his way into the most powerful job on earth but a political operator of some considerable skill, albeit more cunning than strategy.

In winning the presidency – against all odds, according to most opinion polls – Trump not only defied conventionally measured public opinion but reshaped it to his advantage. Like many leaders of the past – and Franklin D. Roosevelt comes most readily to mind – Trump did not simply rely on a narrow power base but built a broad coalition of support – and a most unlikely coalition at that.

Donald Trump was seen by many as erratic, undisciplined, and unmoored, among other things, all of which, to a large extent, were true. But at the same time, it would be unwise to overlook a certain gift for uniting disparate sections of his vast electorate in support of his candidacy, his eventual election in 2016 and in his ensuing presidency.

Trump and his advisers, most notably his onetime chief strategist, Steve Bannon, were, through calculated promotion, able to skilfully tap into a profound sense of alienation from the mores of 21st century America experienced by predominantly low- and middle-income white males, without college degrees. This was a constituency that felt abandoned by the political establishment – a sense of abandonment probably exacerbated by the election in 2008 of a black president (Barack Obama) and the nomination by the Democratic Party in 2016 of a woman (Hillary Clinton) as its candidate for President. Their hitherto perceived status as entitled white males was under siege from a political class from which they felt excluded. For many of these displaced people, government itself had become the enemy – abandoning their communities while, in their view, looking after the interests of minorities, such as African-Americans, Hispanics, women, LGBTQ people and others.

As *New York Times* columnist Charles Blow wrote, Barack Obama wasn't actually on the ballot in 2016, 'but in a way he was'. Trump wasn't only running against Hillary Clinton, he was also running against 'the black shadow of a black man'.

These voters chose the opposite of Obama, they chose the moral and intellectual antithesis, someone who could arrest the advance that Obama represented: an ascension of multicultural power and a coming erasure of white advantage and the dominance of white culture, all of which establishment forces had either allowed or encouraged...Trump was elected to restore the cultural narrative of the primacy of whiteness.[134]

Economically, the situation for these disaffected communities targeted by Trump's appeal had deteriorated sharply with structural changes in the U.S. economy. According to figures from the OECD, between 2000 and 2010, U.S. manufacturing had experienced a sharp downward spiral.[135] The number of manufacturing jobs in the country, which had been relatively stable at 17 million since 1965, declined by one third in that decade, falling by 5.8 million to below 12 million in 2010 (returning to just 12.3 million in 2016). Certainly, the recession of 2007–08 accelerated the disruption, but the causes were also structural, not just financial. There was trouble with capital investment, output, productivity, and trade deficits. Contrary to what many believed, productivity gains due to robotics or automation had not been the cause of manufacturing employment's decline; the sector had been hollowing out.

Along with this this severe economic disruption came a growing social disruption. While most people in the U.S. assumed the nation was becoming one big middle class, instead a working class facing declining incomes came into clear, angry view during the 2016 US presidential election, according to the OECD analysis. The median income of men without a secondary school diploma fell by 20% between 1990 and 2013; for men with secondary school diplomas or some college, median income fell by 13%. The decline of U.S. manufacturing – traditionally a route to the middle class – hit these groups especially hard. There was now a major income inequality problem.

But this demographic cohort – displaced white, blue-collar males – would not alone have delivered him the prize. His tactic was to draw in another powerful group sharing that hostility to government and the political class: the very wealthy, the so-called 1%. To the very wealthy, as well as for big business, government constitutes a tax and regulatory burden on corporate profits and shareholder returns. Trump – himself a member of the plutocracy, although posing as an anti-establishment outsider – alone of the contenders for the Republican nomination understood the politics of that crucial convergence, and how to work it to his advantage. Even after his election, he deployed a range of political tactics to energise and sustain his base, all the while ensuring that his blue-collar supporters did not follow their economic interests (which were certainly not those of Trump and the 1%) by using not just overt appeals to race but the full panoply of identity politics. What remained largely invisible to his blue-collar base, thanks to his distractions, was the fact that the neoliberal capitalist paradigm, which was responsible for exporting many of their jobs, remained as dominant as ever, with Trump delivering tax cuts to the 1% and dismantling much crucial regulation and legislation that protected communities, such as environmental protection, consumer laws and health care.

Trump's appeal to the disaffected was by no means new in America. The working- and middle-class voters who rallied behind Trump were precisely the voters who had originally flocked to the segregationist George Wallace and then to Richard Nixon in 1968; they had also flirted with populists like Ross Perot and Pat Buchanan in the 1990s. Now they had found a champion in Trump.[136]

Analysis of Trump's base showed, in comparison with those who supported other

Republican candidates, that they were older and disproportionately less educated, characterised in one account as the descendants of those white working-class voters who began leaving the Democrats in the 1960s. Certainly, the continued defection of white working-class voters from the Democratic Party was a major factor in Ronald Reagan's victories in 1980 and 1984, and many of the defectors – the so-called 'Reagan Democrats' – refused to return to the Democratic fold even after Reagan left office. The Great Recession (also known as the Global Financial Crisis) had dealt what seemed like the final blow to their economic prospects in an economy and society increasingly tilted towards the upper middle-class and the very rich.[137]

Yet it would be a mistake to see Trump's 2016 success due only to the support of the lesser educated, although this group was solidly behind him. The conventional wisdom that he pitched his appeal at the uneducated and stupid people voted for him does not stand up to analysis. First, he needed to secure the Republican nomination. As someone who had long been regarded as a Democrat, a political maverick and an outsider, this was going to be no easy task.

Before the primaries began in 2016, many commentators had written him off altogether, but they were forced to sit up and take notice in April when the Trump campaign sprung a surprise in the New York Republican primary, with the candidate garnering 61% of the overall vote (the first time he gained over 50%), winning across all demographic groups. While that might have been expected in his home state, it becomes clear, when averaging out his support in all state primaries, that wealthier and better-educated voters formed as big a part of

Trump's support base as those at the lower end of the income and education scales.[138]

On the basis of education, on average, voters with a high-school education or less made up just 16% of the Republican electorate overall and a fifth of his voting base, whereas college graduates and postgraduates accounted for 43% of his support. In terms of income, voters earning under $US50,000 made up 29% of the electorate, accounting for 32% of Trump's support, whereas those earning over $US100,000 accounted for 37% of the electorate and 34% of his base. In Illinois, for example, he took 46% of the vote among low earners, but they made up only a quarter of the electorate, whereas he attracted 39% of the highest earners, who made up two-fifths of that primary's voters.

The political class scoffed at his constantly repeated mantra of making America great again, but evidence suggests this simple slogan resonated with an electorate seeking uplift. According to analysis by the Pew Research Center, two-thirds of Hillary Clinton's supporters were of the view that the next generation would be better off than people are today. But the reverse was true among Trump supporters: 69% thought the next generation would be worse off.[139]

Writing in *The Atlantic*, Andrew McGill called this startling discrepancy in world view a 'hope gap',[140] and it was exploited skilfully by Trump's carefully targeted messages – messages dismissed by many as mere bluster and bombast. Whether they were or not is beside the point: Trump identified an audience hungry for such a message and he delivered – rhetorically, at least – in spades.

Trump's campaign had little to do with facts. And in his avoidance of facts – mixed with his broadsides against elites and the despised 'political class' – he spoke to an audience whose politics was based on gut feelings, nostalgia for a lost world (real or imagined), a vague but strong resentment and an almost indefinable sense of loss. Confused, yes; contradictory, most certainly; ambiguous, definitely. But he spoke a language they understood.

A Question of Legitimacy

Questions of legitimacy, in one form of another, had always troubled Donald Trump. Suggestions that he exaggerated his wealth were met with fierce rejections, even lawsuits. Yet he always refused to make public his tax returns – as every other presidential contender before him had done – presumably because the details might have cast doubt on his legitimacy as a self-proclaimed multi-billionaire. Another concern of his was his place in American society, fuelled by a lifelong resentment that the real establishment of old money, genteel manners and respectability always regarded him as not one of them, an *arriviste*. He knew he did not belong, and Michael Wolff reveals in *Fire and Fury* a moment of unusual candour about Trump's understanding of his own essential nature.

Once, coming back on his plane with a billionaire friend who had brought along a foreign model, Trump, trying to move in on his friend's date, urged a stop in Atlantic City. He would provide a tour of his casino. His friend assured the model that there was nothing to recommend Atlantic City. It was a place overrun by white trash. 'What is this "white trash?"' asked the model. 'They're people just like me', said Trump, 'only they're poor'.[141]

The man Trump succeeded as president, Barack

Obama, was deeply resented by Trump. Obama was everything Trump was not: intelligent, articulate, urbane and gracious. Trump was at the forefront, long before his run for the presidency, in raising issues of legitimacy in regard to the first black president. Trump became the most prominent figure in promoting what was essentially a baseless conspiracy theory – the 'birther movement' – that Obama was not born in the United States and was, therefore, ineligible to serve as president.[142] It is hard to avoid the implied racism here – that a non-white person lacks legitimacy whatever their claims. Part of the 'birther' conspiracy, which held that Obama's birth certificate was a forgery, held that he was also a Muslim – a claim that fanned the flames of anti-Muslim sentiment in the U.S. post 9/11.

However, after he had clinched the Republican nomination in September 2016, as the Trump conceded that 'President Barack Obama was born in the United States. Period', but added the totally false claim that that Hillary Clinton, his opponent in the 2016 U.S. presidential election and one of Obama's opponents in the 2008 Democratic presidential primaries, was responsible for starting the controversy concerning Obama's place of birth.[143]

From the very outset of his own presidency, the question of legitimacy continued to haunt Donald Trump, not only in the eyes of many Americans, but also in his own mind. He trailed his Democratic opponent, Hillary Clinton, in the popular vote by more than 2.8 million votes but won 30 states and 304 votes in the Electoral College to Clinton's 224. He was the fifth American president elected after having lost the popular vote, joining John Quincy Adams (1824), Rutherford B. Hayes (1876), Benjamin Harrison (1888), and George W. Bush (2000). Of the group, Trump had recorded the lowest percentage of the popular vote at just 46.1%.[144] Trump, however, did not accept that he had failed to win the popular vote claiming, without any evidence, that 'millions of people' who voted for Clinton had voted illegally.[145]

A number of senior Democrats refused to attend his inauguration, with many of them citing the circumstances of his election, not just his claim about the popular vote, but also in regard to a controversial announcement late in the campaign that an investigation had been re-opened into Hillary Clinton's use of a non-official email server while serving as Secretary of State, and also claims of Russian involvement in the election in support of Trump. The latter posed a serious dilemma for Trump, especially as further investigation uncovered incontrovertible evidence of Russian involvement (though not necessarily of collusion with the Trump campaign). Despite the seriousness of such a thing having happened, and its implications for national security, he could simply not afford to acknowledge the reality of Russian meddling. Despite mounting evidence, to do so would serve only to further erode his claims to legitimacy.

Among those who publicly raised the issue of legitimacy was the Democratic congressman and respected civil rights leader, John Lewis of Georgia. Speaking on the highly-rated NBC talk show, *Meet the Press*, Lewis had said he would not attend the inauguration because of questions regarding Russia's alleged involvement in manipulating the presidential election, adding that he did not think Trump was a 'legitimate president'. In an angry response, Trump attacked Lewis, claiming that claiming that Lewis's district in Atlanta was 'crime-infested' and that the civil rights hero was 'all talk'. The president-elect's tweets drew outrage from Democratic members of Congress, many of whom praised Lewis's lifelong dedication to fighting for racial equality.[146] Trump's intemperate attack on the revered Lewis opened up another fissure – this time among black Americans – in his perceived legitimacy.

Just days into his presidency, Trump attended a reception at the White House with House and Senate leaders of both parties and senior members of his administration. Trump opened proceedings not with a unifying message or biblical quotation but a blatant lie: 'You know, I won the popular vote.' He then repeated his claim that 'there has been widespread fraud, with three or four million illegal votes for Clinton'. He was immediately called out by the redoubtable Speaker of the House, Nancy Pelosi, who interjected: 'Well, Mr President, that's not true. There's no evidence to support what you just said, and if we're going to work together, we have to stipulate to a certain set of facts.'[147]

A Question of Character

To most Americans, Republican and Democrat alike, John McCain was a revered national hero – a man of valour, courage and with an exemplary record of public service. But not to Donald J. Trump.

Nothing offers such an insight into the character of the 45th president as the animus he directed towards McCain – and, to compound it, coming from someone who most likely had faked, lied and bribed his way out of military service, avoiding the draft for Vietnam. (Trump had even boasted that avoiding sexually transmitted diseases while dating 'is my personal Vietnam'.)[148]

McCain graduated from the U.S. Naval Academy in 1958, receiving a commission in the Navy. He became a naval aviator and flew ground-attack aircraft from aircraft carriers. During the Vietnam War, while on a bombing mission during Operation Rolling Thunder over Hanoi in October 1967, he was shot down, seriously injured, and captured by the North Vietnamese.

Although McCain was seriously wounded and injured, his captors refused to treat him. They beat and interrogated him to get information, and he was given medical care only when the North Vietnamese discovered that his father was an admiral.[149] In mid-1968, his father John S. McCain Jr. was named commander of all U.S. forces in the Vietnam theatre, and the North Vietnamese offered McCain early release for propaganda purposes. McCain refused repatriation unless every man taken in before him was also released. McCain was then placed into solitary confinement, where he remained for two years.[150]

McCain was a prisoner of war until 1973. He sustained wounds that left him with lifelong physical disabilities. His injuries left him permanently incapable of raising his arms above his head. He retired from the Navy as a captain in 1981 and moved to Arizona, where he entered politics.[151]

In 1982, McCain was elected to the House of Representatives, where he served two terms. He entered the Senate in 1987 and easily won re-election five times. While generally adhering to conservative principles, McCain also had a reputation as an independent thinker, unafraid to break from his party on certain issues. In 2008, he ran against Barack Obama as the Republican candidate for president.

In 2015, Trump had this to say about him at a

public rally: '[John McCain is]...not a war hero. He's a war hero – he's a war hero 'cause he was captured. I like people that weren't captured, OK, I hate to tell you.'[152] The remark drew a collective gasp from a nation not yet accustomed to Trump's vitriol and verbal tantrums. The character of the president was now on full view.

In 2018, after a long illness, John McCain died from brain cancer (Trump having cruelly mocked his condition by mimicking an exploding head).[153] Prior to his death, McCain had requested that former presidents George W. Bush and Barack Obama deliver eulogies at his funeral, and asked that both President Donald Trump – from whom he had withdrawn his support after a tape emerged of Trump boasting about his sexual proclivities – and former Alaska Governor and his own vice-presidential running mate in 2008, Sarah Palin, not attend any of the services.[154]

According to reports at the time, Trump had rejected the White House's plans to release a statement praising McCain's life, and he initially said nothing about McCain himself in a tweet that extended condolences to McCain's family.[155] In addition, the flag at the White House, which had been lowered to half-mast the day of McCain's death (25 August), was raised back to full-mast at 12:01 a.m. on 27 August.

Trump was reportedly furious that media coverage of McCain's death was excessive given that McCain had never been president. In contrast with the White House's initial decision, many state governors, both Democratic and Republican, had ordered flags in their states to fly at half-mast until McCain's interment, and Senate leaders Mitch McConnell and Chuck Schumer requested support from the Pentagon so that flags would be flown at half-mast on all government buildings. Following public backlash from the American Legion and Vietnam veterans, Trump later relented, ordering the White House flag back to half-mast later in the day on 27 August. Trump belatedly issued a statement praising McCain's service to the country, and he signed a proclamation ordering flags to be flown at half-mast until McCain's interment at the Naval Academy Cemetery.

Tributes flowed at the funeral – most notably from two former presidents, George W. Bush (Republican) and Barack Obama (Democrat). The current president, pointedly uninvited (and out playing golf), was not mentioned by name, but the implied comparison with the fallen hero was missed by nobody.

Bush praised McCain for his 'courage and decency', an exemplar of the storied American values of standing up to bullying and oppression. 'If we are ever tempted to forget who we are, to grow weary of our cause, John's voice will always come as a whisper over our shoulder — we are better than this, America is better than this', he said. For his part, Obama said:

> So much of our politics, our public life, our public discourse, can seem small and mean and petty, trafficking in bombast and insult, in phony controversies and manufactured outrage. It's a politics that pretends to be brave, but in fact is born of fear. John called us to be bigger than that. He called us to be better than that.[156]

But the most excoriating words came from McCain's daughter, Meghan McCain, whose eulogy drew the sharpest contrast yet between the character if the dead hero and that of the incumbent in the White House.

We gather here to mourn the passing of American greatness — the real thing, not cheap rhetoric from men who will never come near the sacrifice he gave so willingly, nor the opportunistic appropriation of those who lived lives of comfort and privilege while he suffered and served.

Mocking Mr Trump's favourite slogan, she later declared: 'The America of John McCain has no need to be made great again because America was always great.' As the *New York Times* reported, those in attendance then burst out in applause, something that rarely happens during the traditionally solemn funerals held at the cathedral.[157]

The adulation shown towards McCain continued to rankle with Trump. In March 2019 — seven months after his death — Trump issued a series of public statements criticising McCain at least four times in five days.

President Trump claimed credit for John McCain's funeral and complained about not receiving a 'thank you' for the sombre event — even though he had nothing to do with it. He maintained a barrage of attacks critical of McCain for various grievances, the Vietnam War hero's no vote on repealing Obamacare in 2017 and his alerting the FBI to a damning dossier about the President's alleged ties to Russia. Trump also claimed that McCain graduated 'last in his class', though McCain was actually fifth from last.[158] But, speaking at a U.S. Army tank manufacturing plant in Lima, Ohio, Trump also tried out a new anti-McCain tirade that was demonstrably untrue.

> I gave him the kind of funeral that he wanted, which as President I had to approve ... I don't

care about this. I didn't get thank you. That's OK. We sent him on the way, but I wasn't a fan of John McCain.[159]

According to media reports, the audience – many of whom were military veterans – remained quiet during Trump's McCain-bashing monologue. Trump had authorised the use of Air Force 2 to transport McCain's body from Arizona to Washington, D.C., after his death, but the president had nothing to do with his state funeral at the U.S. Capitol on 31 August. Rather, McCain's lying in state was approved via a resolution passed by the Senate.

The President's continuing attacks against the dead senator prompted even some of his most loyal supporters to speak out against him. South Carolina Senator Lindsey Graham told reporters that 'the President's comments about Sen. McCain hurt him more than they hurt the legacy of Sen. McCain Some military veterans were not as measured in their responses. 'Every single senator should speak up regarding their former colleague, Senator McCain. No matter the side. They also should censure POTUS on his latest remarks', retired U.S. Army General Mark Hertling tweeted. 'Anything else is cowardly and speaks to a lack of honor.'[160]

A Sense of Foreboding:
'A world is collapsing before our eyes'

The public denigration of John McCain in 2015 ('not a war hero') was the clearest indication yet of the character of the man running for the Republican nomination, and it sent a stark warning to those whose employment meant they would later have to serve him as president. It marked in a very real sense a turning point in how many people looked at Trump – no longer just the loud, brash outsider, but also a man driven to inordinate lengths by spite and envy. It turned out to be a crucial realisation for some, such as the anonymous senior administration official who first wrote an essay in the *New York Times*, and later a book, *A Warning*, who admitted to being surprised by the lengths to which Trump would go to settle a score, and the way in which he would use his office to seek to limit the nation's recognition of McCain. And it got worse. He (or she) wrote:

> Less than two years into the Trump administration, this episode was almost unremarkable. By then Americans had grown accustomed to the president's pettiness, and they were numb to the endless controversies. Most tried to look the other way. But I couldn't.
>
> I'd spent enough time watching one pointless indignity after another. This one, targeting a veteran and former POW, was the last straw. What did it say about the president? What did it tell us about his values, virtues, and motives? Someone in the administration needed to say something, anything.[161]

This fed into a more general sense of foreboding that had begun to gather even before Trump's inauguration as observers began to take careful note of his erratic pronouncements, uninformed opinions and wild ideas that they had not so long ago been able to dismiss as the babbling of a long-odds contender who would soon fade. Yet, Trump prevailed first in both the Republican race and second in the race for the White House – and that babbling began to be studied. This was about to be

– and very soon became – a presidency quite unlike any other. People were worried, seriously worried.

Just where Trump stood on key issues – and how malleable he might be – was as intriguing to those who became insiders as well as everyone else. Steve Bannon, the right-wing Breitbart News chief who headed Trump's campaign and later became the chief White House strategist and, more controversially, a member of the powerful National Security Council, told *Vanity Fair* magazine in an interview conducted before Trump had secured the nomination in 2016, that Trump was, in terms of a right-wing agenda, a 'blunt instrument for us … I don't know whether he really gets it or not'.[162] (The comment carried echoes of the story, possibly apocryphal, circulating at the time of George W. Bush's candidacy for the Republican nomination for the 2000 election when he was vetted by a group of influential neo-conservatives. 'He is perfect', one was quoted as saying, in reference to Bush's apparent ignorance.)

Given the dominant role of the United States in world affairs, there was considerable trepidation over key issues of foreign policy on which, to many observers, Trump held views that departed significantly from established, largely bipartisan, orthodoxy. Jessica Mathews, the former president of the Carnegie Endowment for International Peace, and a former State Department official, wrote just weeks into the Trump presidency that 'a dangerous moment' had arrived with Trump appearing to dismiss the very fundamentals that had been shared by all three contending school of international relations – the neo-conservatives, liberal internationalists and realists.

Namely, these were, one, a recognition of the

immense value to the security of the United States provided by its allies and associated military and political alliances; two, the belief that the global economy was not a zero-sum competition but rather a mutually beneficial growth system built on open trade and investment; and, three, that dictators had to be tolerated, managed, or confronted, but not admired.

While conceding that Trump's foreign policy often seemed to be a mixture of impulsiveness and ignorance, Mathews pointed to an underlying consistency, citing his 1987 open letter, as a paid announcement in major newspapers, headed 'There's Nothing Wrong with American Foreign Defense Policy That a Little Backbone Can't Cure.' In it, Trump complained that other nations 'have been taking advantage of the United States', convincing the US to pay for their defence while 'brilliantly' managing weak currencies against the dollar.[163]

Donald Trump's thinking, for want of a better term, needed to be taken more seriously than it had, as deeply flawed and illogical as it was.

For a start, he failed to realise, or even understand, how America's global interests had been defended and furthered by its alliances; they had not weakened Uncle Sam so much as enabling him to become such a global colossus. For example, NATO, first and foremost, was initially an anti-Soviet alliance designed to protect American interests and American capital stemming from the post-war Marshall Plan. It was a gross distortion and fanciful in the extreme to represent it as some sort of benevolent organisation funded by the U.S. for the sole benefit of others. But such a distortion played to Trump's political base – and to him this was what mattered.

On the night Trump was elected, France's ambassador to Washington since 2014, Géraud Araud, tweeted:

> It is the end of an era, the era of neoliberalism. We don't yet know what will succeed it … After Brexit and this election, anything is possible. A world is collapsing before our eyes. Vertigo.[164]

The 'dangerous moment' alluded to by Jessica Mathews was not long in coming. Long-term allies of the U.S. suddenly found that the ground had shifted as Trump appeared to be deliberately alienating them, one by one. Immediately after his inauguration, Trump embarked on a series of introductory telephone calls to foreign leaders.

One of his calls was to Australian prime minister Malcolm Turnbull. There was no stronger ally than Australia. Dating back to World War II when the U.S. based its Pacific forces in Australia, the country had dutifully followed America into Korea, Vietnam, the Gulf, Iraq and Afghanistan. Its bond with the U.S. was exemplified by 1960s prime minister Harold Holt's slogan of support for the Vietnam policy of President Lyndon Johnson – 'all the way with LBJ'.

Things started to wrong very early. Turnbull pressed Trump on whether he would follow through on a deal to resettle refugees that had previously been agreed between the two countries. 'This deal will make me look terrible', Trump reportedly told him. 'I think it is a horrible deal, a disgusting deal that I would have never made.' Turnbull, according to the leaked transcript, tried to reason with him but Trump shut down the conversation. 'I have had it. I have been making these calls all day, and this is the most unpleasant call all day.' Then he hung up.[165]

Australia was not alone. The leaders of Canada, the United Kingdom, France, and Germany – the nations comprising the very cornerstones of the American global alliance – were mocked, snubbed, and gratuitously insulted. Unsurprisingly, the diplomatic community was quick to notice the abrupt change with the UK ambassador in Washington, for example, calling the president 'unpredictable' and the Trump White House 'dysfunctional'. Trump, as is his wont, hit back, calling the ambassador 'a very stupid guy', 'wacky' and 'a pompous fool'.[166]

7.

In the Court of King Donald

Let's fucking kill him! ... Let's go in. Let's kill the fucking lot of them. – Donald J. Trump[167]

No external force can ameliorate his attraction to wrongdoing. His presidency is continually jeopardized by it, and so are America's institutions.
– Anonymous[168]

Nothing stays the same for very long in the Trump White House; it is a kaleidoscopic montage of the improbable and the absurd, forever in flux.

An erratic, tantrum-prone president rules like an absolutist monarch of old, governed only by whim and fiat of the moment. He strongly resembles the Queen of Hearts character from the 1865 book *Alice's Adventures in Wonderland* by Lewis Carroll. She is a cruel, foul-tempered woman, given to sudden rages and what Carroll describes as 'blind fury'. She is quick to pronounce death sentences at the slightest offence, real or imagined, often with the phrase, 'off with his/her head!'

Despite the frequency of death sentences, few people are actually beheaded. The King of Hearts quietly pardons many of his subjects when the Queen is not looking, and her soldiers humour her but do not carry out her orders. Such is the situation in the Trump White House: orders are given, but not always carried out; they are often simply forgotten after that.

Courtiers would come and go, falling in and out of favour. If there was a problem at any time, Trump's instinctive reaction was to fire someone.[169] Trust was minimal or non-existent. Trump was always suspicious of those around him, relationships quickly souring as he came to believe that his staff was profiting at his expense. As Michael Wolff observed, Trump was convinced that everyone was greedy like he was and that sooner or later they would try to take what was rightfully his.[170]

A senior official characterised a typical cabinet-level session with the president as being given orders of which one-third were 'flat out stupid', another third impossible to implement or would not solve the problem in hand, and the other third simply 'flat-out illegal'.[171]

The situation had more than just passing resemblance to a monarchy of old. The installation of his family, daughter Ivanka Trump and her husband, Jared Kushner, in key advisory positions, answerable only to him, thwarted any attempt at bringing a rational process to the activity of executive government. For example, Trump put Kushner in charge of brokering peace in the Israeli–Palestinian conflict, despite the fact that Kushner had no foreign policy experience or experience in the Middle East. After advising her father in an unofficial capacity for the first two months of his administration, Ivanka Trump was later appointed 'First Daughter and Senior Advisor to the President'.[172] Both attracted criticism for retaining their extensive business interests, adding another layer of complexity to the intrigues of the court.

Adults in the room

Very early in the Trump administration – or even before the inauguration – two things were clear: experience in government and even knowledge of how government worked were noticeably lacking; and the new president was both impulsive and dangerously uninformed. Six months into Trump's presidency, it was reported that Defence Secretary James Mattis and then-Homeland Security Secretary John Kelly, both former generals, had made a pact that one of them had to be in the United States at all times, presumably for the purpose of stopping the president from doing something dangerous.[173] They were joined informally by Secretary of State Rex Tillerson and National Security Advisor H. R. McMaster, often referred to as 'the adults in the room'.

The 'adults in the room' quickly became a familiar trope in the Trump presidency, accurately depicting the more responsible members of his inner circle who struggled daily to restrain an impulsive and erratic commander-in-chief with a minimal attention span and an aversion to reading briefing papers, even when they had been reduced to dot points. As chief of staff, John Kelly worked hard to arrange briefings from experts on a range of topics considered vital for the President of the United States to know about, but Trump was often bored. At one point when Kelly proposed a subject briefing, Trump told him: 'I don't want to talk to anyone. I know more than they do. I know better than anybody else.'[174]

The efforts of the adults were complemented by

other senior officials, who were dubbed 'the Steady State' – intent on using their influence to, as one insider put it, 'keep the wheels coming off the White House wagon'.[175] But as time wore on, it became clear that restraint was nigh impossible. Frustrated officials even considered a mass resignation to draw the public's attention to the disarray at the top. As one official wrote:

We realized as year two wore on that we couldn't rely on any system to instil in the president the leadership traits he'd never developed. We returned to running interference against gross impulsivity, confronting each third-rate presidential contrivance as it came and trying to make the best of it.[176]

'Off with their heads'

A feature of the Trump White House was the rapid turnover of key staff. The tone was set just days into the presidency when Trump fired acting Attorney-General, Sally Yates, after she questioned the legality of Trump's travel ban on seven Muslim-majority countries. Yates, who was appointed by Barack Obama, believed it discriminated unconstitutionally against Muslims, and ordered justice department lawyers not to enforce the president's executive order. She had lasted just ten days.

After twenty-three days, out went National Security Advisor, Michael Flynn. Technically, Flynn resigned, but he was asked to do so by the president. His departure followed weeks of deepening scandal in which it emerged that he had misled White House officials, including the vice-president, over his contact with Russian ambassador Sergei Kislyak. Then followed FBI director James Comey, press secretary Sean Spicer, and FBI deputy director Andrew McCabe. Over time, many others would follow. Most notably Veterans' Affairs Secretary David Shulkin, Attorney-General Jeff Sessions, Homeland Security Secretary Kirstjen Nielsen, assistant Attorney-General Rod Rosenstein, Labour Secretary Alexander Acosta, and Director of National Intelligence Dan Coats, among others. No one was safe.

After his acquittal by the Senate in his impeachment trial, Trump hit back at those he blamed for helping bring it about, firing a subpoenaed witness, Lieutenant-Colonel Alexander Vindman, from his job at the National Security Council, and another witness, ambassador Gordon Sondland. He later dismissed Michael K. Atkinson, the Inspector General of the Intelligence Community, describing Atkinson as disloyal for his role in forwarding the whistleblower complaint which led to Trump's impeachment over asking the Ukraine president to investigate a political rival as a condition of receiving already legislated military aid.[177] Over next six weeks in April–May 2020, Trump fired four more inspectors-general of cabinet departments, in several cases over actions which Trump disliked, widely seen as 'retaliation'.[178]

But the departures that had the most impact were those seen as the 'adults' most able to restrain the commander-in-chief – Secretary of State Rex Tillerson; the generals John Kelly, H. R. McMaster, and James Mattis; the economics adviser Gary Cohn; and the senior Republican Reince Priebus. Each in his own way had sought to restrain or modify Trumpian excesses; despite occasional victories, they did not succeed in producing lasting change. Other powerful figures who sought to harness

Trump to their own agendas, such as strategist Steve Bannon and National Security Adviser John Bolton, were also discarded along the way.

Rex Tillerson

Rex Tillerson served as Trump's Secretary of State from the start of the administration until 31 March 2018. An engineer by training, he had been CEO of the energy giant ExxonMobil, one of the world's biggest corporations. He had spent his entire working life at the company, rising through the ranks to the very top. He later became president of the Boy Scouts of America, during which time the organisation decided to allow gay members to join for the first time.

It was an unorthodox call to appoint Tillerson to such a high-profile post, given that he had had no experience working in government. But to Trump, who liked appearances, the big, bluff Texan with a commanding presence looked the part he would play on the world stage. Further, the appointment sent a strong signal to the business community that the administration would be mindful of its interests and have an inside voice. Trump drew attention to Tillerson's experience in dealings with Russia and Saudi Arabia, hailing him as a 'world-class player and dealmaker' and 'one of the truly great business leaders of the world'.[179] His close adviser, Kellyanne Conway, described the choice for the top cabinet post as 'very Trumpian-inspired', and said on television he would have a 'big impact'.[180]

It was not a happy relationship. Tillerson, the hard-headed businessman long accustomed to running his own show, very quickly found the chaos of the Trump White House very different from the orderly and rational structures of the corporate boardroom. Inevitably, tensions soon erupted over both temperament and issues, and within months there were ongoing rumours that Tillerson was on the way out.

In one oft-reported clash, Trump berated a handful of senior military people at a top-level meeting at the Pentagon, questioning why the United States couldn't get some oil as payment for the troops it had deployed there. 'We spent $7 trillion; they're ripping us off. Where is the fucking oil?' Then he began railing at the lack of apparent progress in the protracted war in Afghanistan. 'You're all losers ... You don't know how to win anymore ... I wouldn't go to war with you people ...You're a bunch of dopes and babies.'[181]

Tillerson and the senior military commanders were stunned. Tillerson, whose father and grandfather had both served in the military, was particularly aggrieved about trying to make money out of U.S. troops, and was the lone voice to speak up, telling Trump he was ' ... just wrong. Mr President, you're totally wrong. None of that is true ... The men and women who put on a uniform don't do it to become soldiers of fortune. That's not why they put on a uniform and go out and die ... They do it to protect our freedom.'

The meeting ended shortly after and Trump left. Standing outside the meeting room with a small group of people, Tillerson let fly: 'He's a fucking moron.'[182] Tillerson considered resigning, but was dissuaded by White House chief of staff, Reince Priebus, who called him to come and talk about it. Tillerson told him: 'I just don't like the way the president talks to these generals. They don't deserve it. I can't sit around and listen to this from the president. He's just a moron.'[183]

Tillerson did not resign but having publicly confronted Trump – and having pointedly refused to deny he had called him a 'fucking moron' – his days were clearly numbered. He had been 'hard' with the president, according to Reince Priebus, and Trump did not like hard.[184]

Tillerson's role was made more difficult by the involvement of the president's son-on-law, Jared Kushner, in foreign negotiations. One evening, Tillerson was out to dinner in Washington when the restaurant owner asked if he would like to say hello to the Mexican Foreign Minister, who also happened to be at the same establishment. As they walked to the back of the restaurant Tillerson was shocked to find the minister, who Tillerson did not know was in town, dining with Kushner.[185]

In March 2018, Tillerson was fired – by presidential tweet as he returned from a trip to Africa. He would later say of his time in the post:

> What was challenging for me coming from the disciplined, highly process-oriented ExxonMobil corporation ... [was] to go to work for a man who is pretty undisciplined, doesn't like to read, doesn't read briefing reports, doesn't like to get into the details of a lot of things, but rather just kind of says, 'This is what I believe.'[186]

In response, Trump called Tillerson 'dumb as a rock' and 'lazy as hell'.[187] Tillerson was succeeded by CIA director Mike Pompeo.

Reince Priebus

Reince Priebus served as White House Chief of Staff for President Donald Trump from his inauguration until 31 July 2017. He had served as the chairman of the Republican National Committee (RNC) from 2011 to 2017, and his translation to the White House was designed to assuage many Republicans who remained wary of Trump. As chairman, Priebus was the public face of the party and frequently criticised the policies of President Barack Obama. He presided over the Republican Party during the 2012 and 2016 presidential elections. Priebus had publicly criticised Trump during the early stages of the 2016 Republican presidential primaries, but later called for party unity. He opposed efforts to deny Trump the nomination at the 2016 Republican National Convention and supported his presidential campaign in the general election.

His presence was seen as a guarantee of orthodoxy, and he was regarded by party leaders as having the most capable set of hands among Trump's aides.[188] However, less than seven months later he was gone, recording the shortest tenure of anyone in the senior White House role.

A lawyer by training, Priebus set about installing former RNC staffers and other trusted figures in key roles, while he and Steve Bannon, along with vice-president Mike Pence, focused on cabinet positions. But the methodical ways Priebus brought with him from the RNC did not necessarily translate into the White House where three key players competed for influence – Priebus, Bannon, and Trump's son-in-law, Jared Kushner in a unique arrangement in which they shared co-equal status at the top of the organisational chart.[189] It was a recipe for chaos.

While Priebus sought to manage as best he could – and his attempts at controlling access to the president ruffled feathers – his authority was limited. Bannon did what he wanted, Kushner and his wife,

Ivanka, worked as free agents with unfettered access to Trump, and Trump himself simply refuse to be organised. While Bannon would later concede that Priebus was in charge, the Kushners simply by-passed him. 'You don't think they should be here?' Trump asked several times. No, they should not, Priebus said. But nothing happened.[190]

Tensions in the White House began to be reported in the news media, an accusations of leaking inflamed the situation. As Priebus struggled to bring order to bear, a meeting in his office flared into ugly confrontation when Bannon clashed with the president's daughter, telling her she was 'nothing but a fucking staffer', and like everyone else she, too, had to work through Priebus. Ivanka fired back: 'I'm not a staffer...I'll never be a staffer. I'm the first daughter … and I'm never going to be a staffer.'[191] It was an impossible situation, and Priebus was on the losing end: he was unceremoniously fired in a presidential tweet announcing the appointment of John Kelly as chief of staff.[192] Kelly was taken aback by the brutality of the announcement, but Priebus, who could read Trump, said it made sense once it was understood how Trump made decisions: 'The president has zero psychological ability to recognize empathy or pity in any way.'[193]

Although they parted on reasonably good terms, the reality was that Trump never trusted him; Priebus never had the authority of a true chief of staff. Rather than being empowered to make decisions and to speak on the president's behalf, as one commentator noted, 'he played the part of a nervous courtier, always hovering around the boss in an attempt to curry favor, always scrambling to clean up messes he was powerless to prevent.'[194]

Months after he left the White House, as Bob

Woodward wrote, Priebus made a final assessment which went to the heart of how the court of King Donald functioned: he believed he had been surrounded in the West Wing by 'high-ranking natural killers' with no experience in government and no requirement to produce regular work products, such as a plan, a speech, the outline of a strategy, a budget, a daily and weekly schedule. They were 'roving interlopers, a band of chaos creators', he said specifically naming Ivanka Trump, Jared Kushner, adviser Kellyanne Conway and Steve Bannon 'a strategist in an operation that had none'. Their discussions, said Priebus, were not designed to persuade but, like their president, 'to win – to slay, crush and demean'.[195]

John Kelly

John Kelly, a retired U.S. Marine Corps general, served as the White House chief of staff from 31 July 2017 to 2 January 2019. He had previously served as Secretary of Homeland Security in the Trump administration where his firm hand had impressed Trump. Kelly brought a stern presence to the White House. But Trump found Kelly hard to read, even asking people if Kelly liked him. 'Does he ever smile?' Trump once asked.[196]

The chaos in the White House was alien to Kelly, whose whole working life had been spent in an environment of tight discipline, clearly defined roles and responsibilities, and an acknowledged chain of command. Kelly, though, knew what he was getting into, having privately criticised the disorder to Trump, saying he believed he could straighten the place out.[197] He was wrong.

Kelly walked into a hornets' nest. His first task was to fire communications director, Anthony Scaramucci, the flamboyant New York financier, who had been brought in largely at the urging of Jared Kushner and Ivanka Trump, to counter Priebus whose efforts to rein them in they had resented. Scaramucci had given a scathing interview to *New Yorker* magazine, unloading on the state of internal politics at the White House.[198] He had lasted just eleven days in the job.

But the task ahead for Kelly was daunting. Bannon posed a serious problem, but even more serious was the problem of the president's family, who, with their privileged access to Trump and influence on him, constituted a rival centre of power within the West Wing and, as such, undermined Kelly's attempts to restore order. Jared and Ivanka, as Michael Wolff noted, had become adept at wielding and guarding their power; they were 'a fearsome presence'.[199] It made the task of managing the president that much harder; they had his ear, they had influence with him. Indeed, when Kelly attempted to raise the issue with the president, seeking to clarify their roles, he found Trump not only reluctant to acknowledge a problem, but actually delighted with their work, even seeing in Kushner a future Secretary of State.[200]

Not a year into the job, Kelly began to be the subject of speculation, clearly fed from the White House, that he was rapidly losing influence with the president. One former administration official was quoted as saying that Kelly had 'ruled the West Wing with an iron fist' during the first six months of his tenure but added that was no longer the case; another official spoke of Kelly's waning influence and his frustration at not being able to manage

Trump. Numerous sources noted that Kelly's wider efforts to restrict the number of people who had access to the president sat uneasily with the way Trump had managed his business empire for decades.[201]

By the end of 2018, it was clear Kelly was about to go, and the president announced just that on 6 December. The *New York Times* reported Kelly had 'lent a patina of respectability to a White House that at the time was staffed almost entirely by people who had never before served in government.' However, it noted that despite his imposing military credentials, Kelly slowly had come to realise the futility of trying to control the president, and 'ultimately resigned himself to a stalemate of coexistence, simply letting Trump be Trump and complaining to his colleagues about how miserable he was in the job.'[202] He was succeeded by budget director Mick Mulvaney, in an acting capacity.

H. R. McMaster

H. R. [Herbert Raymond] McMaster was not a good fit in the Trump White House. McMaster had served in the Gulf War and was later a military history professor at the U.S. Military Academy from 1994 to 1996. He had also been a research fellow at the Hoover Institution, a member of the Council on Foreign Relations and a Consulting Senior Fellow at the International Institute for Strategic Studies. His PhD thesis was critical of American strategy and military leadership during the Vietnam War and served as the basis for his acclaimed book, *Dereliction of Duty*, which was widely read in the United States military.

McMaster was a serious man in a hostile environment where expertise was regarded with suspicion at best or even outright derision. He was on collision course from day one when he was named to succeed Michael Flynn, who had been dismissed for lying about Russian contacts during the 2016 campaign.

The White House was in damage control, losing Flynn just days after Trump's inauguration, and Steve Bannon had suggested a senior military figure and came up with McMaster, considered 'a renegade and an outsider in the Army club'. Bannon knew McMaster's reputation as a scholar and advised him not to lecture the president, telling him 'he doesn't like intellectuals'. He also advised him to wear his uniform to the interview with Trump. McMaster disregarded the advice: talking for twenty minutes and wearing a suit. According to Bannon's account, Trump asked after the interview: 'Who was that guy? He wrote a book didn't he? It said bad things about people, I thought you told me he was in the Army...He's dressed like a beer salesman.'[203]

After several others were interviewed, McMaster was invited back for a second interview, this time wearing his uniform. Trump was impressed and immediately offered him the job, shaking McMaster's hand and saying: 'Get the media. Get the cameras in here.' As Bob Woodward noted, Trump wanted a picture with his latest general who looked straight out of Central Casting. Introducing McMaster, Trump said: 'He's a man of tremendous talent and tremendous experience.'[204]

The gloss soon began to fade. McMaster was widely respected in foreign policy circles and was very much his own man (a dangerous disposition in the Trump White House). At the first town-hall meeting of National Security Council staff after being appointed in February 2017, McMaster let it be known that as a non-partisan army officer he did not vote. This unwittingly sent a message to Trump, who demanded political loyalty from everyone in his administration; to not be for him was to be against him.[205]

Just six weeks into his tenure, Syrian aircraft dropped deadly sarin gas on civilians in an attack on the rebel-held town of Khan Sheikhoun, and McMaster sought to brief Trump on an American response – but the president was not listening. To both Kushner and McMaster, it appeared that the president was more annoyed about having to think about the attack than by the attack itself.[206] He was annoyed that McMaster was burdening him with so much detail. As Woodward noted, McMaster's briefing style was all wrong for Trump: order and discipline, hierarchy and linear thinking. So frustrated was Trump that when McMaster appeared at the Oval Office for scheduled meetings, the president would say: 'You again? I just saw you.'[207] Trump would later go on to openly mock McMaster's briefing style in front of meetings, which distressed National Security Council staff. One was reported as saying: 'The president doesn't fire people ... He just tortures them until they're willing to quit.'[208]

It was inevitable that McMaster would go. It was not just the constant humiliation from Trump but differences over major policy issues, such as Russia, Syria and Iran that drove home the hopelessness of his attempts to restrain the impulsiveness of a president who refused to listen, refused to read, refused to learn.

On 22 March 2018, McMaster resigned.[209] Although the departure was ostensibly amicable, McMaster was quoted as having privately called Trump 'a dope'.[210] He was succeeded by John Bolton.

James Mattis

James Mattis was a former general in the Marines, having seen active service in the Gulf War, Afghanistan and Iraq. He served as Secretary of Defence from January 2017 to January 2019. Although highly regarded as a military leader, it was not the substance that informed Trump's appointment of Mattis so much as the appearance – the upright military bearing and especially the nickname, 'Mad Dog', which Mattis personally disliked. In any case, the appointment was reassuring to the national security establishment.[211] While expressing reservations about a retired general running the Pentagon, respected defence commentator Thomas E. Ricks, writing in *Foreign Policy*, noted that if it had to be a general then Mattis was 'a good choice. He is a rarity in that he is a genuine strategic thinker, pushing himself and others to stretch their minds. This tendency is not always welcomed.'[212]

Mattis was generally credited with bringing stability and professionalism to his role, and for a time he was successful in reining in the president's wilder ideas, such as ordering the assassination of the Syrian president, Bashar al-Assad, in an air strike after the sarin gas attack in April 2017. Yes, Mattis told Trump. He would get right on it. But hanging up the phone, he told an aide: 'We're not going to do any of that. We're going to be much more measured.' His team then went onto develop small, medium, and large options for a conventional air strike – the standard three tiers of response.[213]

Mattis had reasonable success in managing the president despite relatively minor skirmishes on issues such as the defence arrangement with South Korea and troop commitments in Afghanistan. However, the relationship was to fracture spectacularly when Trump announced, quite contrary to his administration's stated policy, that he would withdraw all American troops from Syria, where they were fighting the Islamic State. To say Mattis was affronted is an understatement: This sudden (and ultimately reversed) policy shift posed a dire challenge to his core beliefs. He had spent much of his career as a fighter in the Middle East. He had battled Islamist extremists and understood the danger they represented. He believed that a retreat from Syria would threaten the security of American troops elsewhere in the region, and would especially threaten America's allies in the anti-ISIS coalition. These allies would, in Mattis's view, feel justifiably betrayed by Trump's decision.

Next day, Mattis met Trump in the Oval Office, making his case for keeping troops in Syria. Trump rejected his arguments. Thirty minutes into the conversation, Mattis told the president, 'You're going to have to get the next secretary of defense to lose to ISIS. I'm not going to do it.' He handed Trump his letter of resignation.[214] In it, Mattis wrote:

My views on treating allies with respect and also being clear-eyed about both malign actors and strategic competitors are strongly held and informed by over four decades of immersion in these issues. We must do everything possible to advance an international order that is most conducive to our security, prosperity and values, and we are strengthened in this effort by the solidarity of our alliances.

Because you have the right to have a Secretary of Defense whose views are better aligned with yours on these and other subjects, I believe it is right for me to step down from my position.[215]

Mattis wrote that his resignation would be effective 28 February 2019, but three days later Trump moved his departure date up to 1 January, after becoming angered by the implicit criticism of Trump's worldview in Mattis's letter.[216] Mattis was succeeded by Mark Esper.

In 2020, as the United States was convulsed by protests after the death of yet another black man at the hands of white police, Mattis publicly berated Trump for deliberately trying to cause division among the American people, and for advocating military action to 'dominate' the protests in the country. He wrote that Trump was 'the first president in my lifetime who does not try to unite the American people' and that America is 'witnessing the consequences of three years without mature leadership'. He called for accountability for 'those in office who would make a mockery of our Constitution'.[217]

Gary Cohn

Gary Cohn served as Director of the National Economic Council and chief economic advisor to President Donald Trump from 2017 to 2018, managing and overseeing the administration's economic policy agenda. Before serving in the White

House, Cohn was president and chief operating officer of investment bank Goldman Sachs, where he worked for more than 25 years. His reputation was seen as invaluable in reassuring Wall Street about the economic bona fides of the administration. An avowed globalist, he was also seen as an effective foil for the anti-globalist economic nationalism of Trump and his circle.

Cohn's recruitment owed much to Trump's son-in-law Jared Kushner who, in the peculiar value system of the family, liked to mention that the president of Goldman Sachs was working for him. Trump himself also exploited the connection, constantly pulling Cohn into meetings, especially with foreign leaders, just to introduce him as the former president of Goldman Sachs.[218]

Cohn was instrumental in driving the tax cuts legislation of 2017, a key plank in Trump's policy platform. But it was the level of intervention on contentious issues that highlighted Cohn's self-appointed role in the White House: to save Trump from himself.

Bob Woodward described how Trump had become obsessed with the trade agreement with South Korea, seeing it as working against U.S. interests and intent on unilaterally cancelling it, even having a letter drafted to that effect to the South Korean president. Trump was furious that the U.S. had an $18 billion annual trade deficit with South Korea but was spending $3.5 billion a year to keep American troops there. The point of the American presence was to be able to detect within seven seconds the launching of missiles from North Korea; the equivalent capability in Alaska took 15 minutes. As Bob Woodward wrote, it represented the essence of national security – but Trump could not see beyond the trade balance sheet.[219]

'I can stop this', Cohn reportedly told an aide who had expressed concern about possible consequences with other trading partners. Cohn, who clearly understood the security implications, simply removed the letter, already prepared for signing, from the president's desk. He knew that without it sitting in front of him he would soon forget it. Cohn was right.[220]

Cohn was increasingly uneasy about many aspects of the Trump presidency, and when Trump refused to condemn violence by white supremacists at a rally in Charlottesville, Virginia, in August 2017, when a car was driven into protestors, killing a woman, Cohn considered resigning. He publicly voiced his concern, saying he believed the administration could do better in 'consistently and unequivocally condemning' white supremacists.[221]

On 6 March 2018, Cohn announced his intention to resign; the trigger was Trump's proposal to impose import tariffs on steel and aluminium, which ran counter to Cohn's free trade principles and against his advice. Trump had peremptorily cancelled a meeting that Cohn arranged for him with companies that use steel and aluminium in their products, in an effort to dissuade the president from imposing the tariffs.[222] He was succeeded by Larry Kudlow.

Steve Bannon

Steve Bannon served as White House chief strategist during the first seven months of Trump's term, having earlier played the key strategic role in his 2016 campaign. He had been a naval officer, media executive, political strategist, investment banker, and the former executive chairman of *Breitbart News*, a right-wing online news website. He was the ideologue in the White House primarily concerned with keeping the president in touch with his electoral base.

When a Trump aide first sounded out Bannon and told him Trump was thinking about running for president, an incredulous Bannon replied: 'Of what country?'[223] But Bannon, a soldier of fortune, soon came to see Trump as a vehicle for his own political agenda; he was keenly aware of Trump's charismatic appeal to the political right, the Tea Party movement, and the Internet meme base.[224] It was Bannon who harnessed Trump's campaign to the final phase of a populist insurgency that had been gathering momentum up in America for years. Initially sceptical of Trump's chances of victory in 2016, Bannon – who was under no illusion about Trump's many limitations and shortcomings – was the one true believer in the Trump camp, and Trump credited him with almost mystical powers. He was also the only insider able to offer a coherent vision of Trump's populism.[225]

But Bannon had enemies, including most orthodox Republicans. Trump's brief flirtation with making Bannon his chief of staff was quickly shot down. Media tycoon Rupert Murdoch told Trump it would be a dangerous choice; TV host and former Republican congressman Joe Scarborough warned Trump that 'Washington will go up in flames' if Bannon became chief of staff.[226] Instead, Trump made him chief strategist, a new post, that put him on co-equal footing with the man he made chief of staff, Reince Priebus. Controversially, Trump appointed him to the National Security Council's Principals Committee, a Cabinet-level senior interagency forum for considering national security issues, but it lasted only a few weeks before he was removed.

Bannon fought for traction in the White House, especially against Jared Kushner and Ivanka Trump whose influence on the president he saw as running counter to what he had laid out. Just where the relationship fractured is hard to pinpoint, but Trump had resented a book by journalist Joshua Green extolling Bannon's role in the campaign,[227] and was angered by what he saw as Bannon's rising profile and the suggestion that he owed his success to him, in part triggered by a cover in *Time* magazine in February depicting Bannon as 'The Great Manipulator'. Bannon, for his part, sensed trouble was brewing, telling Green: 'Trump doesn't like any co-stars', and pushing unsuccessfully to have the publication of Green's book pushed back.

Joshua Green had no illusions about Bannon and knew his White House tenure would be short.

Bannon's role in the White House had always struck me as a tenuous affair. He was a bomb-thrower and an outsider with no previous experience in operating the levers in government, a man with perhaps more enemies than anyone in Washington, and someone whose habit it was to feud bitterly with those he disagreed with. Further, he was a radical with a grandiose plan to transform politics – not just in the United States, but across the globe. Something had to give.[228]

The day the book appeared, the *Washington Post* reported that Trump was upset by Bannon's participation in a book 'particularly a cover photo giving equal billing to Trump and his chief strategist'.

Every time Green was on CNN, where he is

now a contributor, Trump grew unhappy with his references to Bannon as a thinker and strategist – and upset that the conversation was not instead about Trump.[229]

Trump blamed Bannon for the fallout from the Charlottesville protests in August 2017. The Unite the Right rally degenerated into violence and acrimony, and a protestor was killed. Republicans and Democrats alike condemned the actions of white nationalists, neo-Nazis and alt-right activists, but as the *New York Times* pointed out, Trump was equivocal, 'the only national political figure to spread blame for the "hatred, bigotry and violence" that resulted in the death of one person to "many sides".' [230] The decision to blame 'many sides' was reported to have been taken by Bannon.[231]

The National Association for the Advancement of Colored People (NAACP) issued a statement saying that while they 'acknowledge and appreciate President Trump's disavowment of the hatred which has resulted in a loss of life today' they called on him 'to take the tangible step to remove Steve Bannon – a well-known white supremacist leader – from his team of advisers'. The statement further described Bannon as a 'symbol of white nationalism' who 'energized that sentiment' through his position within the White House.[232]

Bannon's employment in the White House ended less than a week later, with speculation as to whether he was fired or if he resigned. In an official statement, the White House said: 'John Kelly and Steve Bannon have mutually agreed today would be Steve's last day. We are grateful for his service and wish him the best.'[233] He was not replaced.

John Bolton

John Bolton served as National Security Advisor from April 2018 to September 2019. He was far and away the most experienced hand in the Trump White House in terms of government experience, having served as an Assistant Attorney-General under President Ronald Reagan from 1985 to 1989, an Assistant Secretary of State for International Organization Affairs under President George H. W. Bush from 1989 to 1993 and Under Secretary of State for Arms Control and International Security Affairs under President George W. Bush from 2001 to 2005. He also served as the U. S. Ambassador to the United Nations from 2005 to 2006.

A noted hawk on foreign policy and a strong neo-conservative, Bolton had been initially overlooked for the position of National Security Adviser in favour of H. R. McMaster after Michael Flynn was sacked in 2017. According to Steve Bannon, who was pushing for Bolton, Trump did not like Bolton's moustache, adding: 'Trump doesn't think he looks the part.'[234]

When later named to succeed McMaster, Bolton wasted no time in making his mark, ordering significant staff cuts at the National Security Council,[235] and persuading Trump to withdraw from the nuclear deal with Iran negotiated under the Obama administration.[236] In his role, Bolton abandoned the kinds of internal policy debates that his predecessor McMaster had in place. *The New York Times* reported that this change in practices contributed to Trump's sudden decision to withdraw the U. S. from Syria in January 2019, prompting the resignation of defence secretary James Mattis.[237] Clearly, Bolton was gaining in influence, but tensions were mounting.

Trump appeared to be reining in Bolton. By May 2019, Trump had undercut some of Bolton's hard line positions, stating he was not seeking regime change in Iran and contradicting Bolton's correct assertion that North Korea had recently violated United Nations resolutions by testing new short-range missiles.[238] On 10 September, President Trump claimed on Twitter that he had told Bolton 'services are no longer needed' given the 'many' between the two. Bolton resigned next day.[239]

In 2020, Bolton released a scathing memoir,[240] which the White House sought unsuccessfully to suppress, detailing his seventeen months with Trump. In an interview, Bolton expanded on revelations in the book, which he argued supports his claims that Trump was 'unfit for office' and lacked the 'competence to carry out the job'. Describing the president as 'erratic and impulsive', Bolton slammed Trump's handling of U.S. foreign policy, accusing him of prioritising re-election and personal relationships over the country's national security. Bolton highlighted Trump's dealings with North Korea, Russia, China and Ukraine as prime examples.

Bolton said his book showed 'a pattern quite contrary to the image [Trump] would like to convey, of a decisive president who knows something about what he's doing.' He noted that Trump 'very rarely read much' during intelligence briefings and said Trump was unwilling 'to do systematic learning so that he could make the most informed decisions'.[241] In response, on the eve of the book's publication, Trump tweeted that Bolton was 'a liar and grossly incompetent'.[242] Bolton was succeeded by Robert O'Brien.

It was always going to be a wild ride under the Trump presidency. His recklessness, total lack of experience, and unwillingness to learn all sent strong warning signals to the old hands in government, whose duty it was to operate and protect the key institutions on which government and the rule of law depend. These men and women, whose task it was to speak truth to power, took a collective deep breath and braced for action. They had every reason to be confident that they would prevail against the neophyte, as George Packer wrote in *The Atlantic*:

> The new president was impetuous, bottomlessly ignorant, almost chemically inattentive, while the bureaucrats were seasoned, shrewd, protective of themselves and their institutions. They knew where the levers of power lay and how to use them or prevent the president from doing so. Trump's White House was chaotic and vicious, unlike anything in American history, but it didn't really matter as long as 'the adults' were there to wait out the president's impulses and deflect his worst ideas and discreetly pocket destructive orders lying around on his desk.[243]

James Baker, the former general counsel of the FBI, told Packer that many government officials, himself included, went into the administration convinced that they were either smarter than the president, or that they could hold their own against him, or that they could protect the institution because they understood the rules and regulations and how the system was supposed to work. He had hoped they could defend the institution that they loved or served against what they perceived to be 'the inappropriate actions of the president'.

They were so wrong! He added: 'And I think they are fooling themselves. They're fooling themselves. He's light-years ahead of them.'

The 'adults' were quite incapable of seeing what Packer described as Trump's special political talents – 'his instinct for every adversary's weakness, his fanatical devotion to himself, his knack for imposing his will, his sheer staying power'. They had also failed to appreciate that they were part of the hated 'political class' at which Trump's populist-roused ire was directed; they were part of the swamp that had to drained. Packer goes on to note further that they failed to grasp 'the readiness of large numbers of Americans to accept, even relish, Trump's contempt for democratic norms and basic decency'.

***

It took the arrival of such a leader to reveal how many things that had always seemed engraved in monumental stone turned out to depend on those flimsy norms, and how much the norms depended on public opinion. Their vanishing exposed the real power of the presidency. Legal precedent could be deleted with a keystroke; law enforcement's independence from the White House was optional; the separation of powers turned out to be a gentleman's agreement; transparent lies were more potent than solid facts.

None of this, Packer writes, was clear to the political class until Trump became president. Then it was on full display, each day, every day, in the court of King Donald. Trump could not hide his contempt for those he saw as trying to thwart him as well as the institutions designed to check absolute power. He would destroy anyone or anything standing in his way.

Something valuable had been taken for granted; now it was gone. Would America ever be the same again?

Notes

1 Originally appeared in *Canberra Times* and *Sydney Morning Herald*, 12 December 2016, as 'Trump the punk rocker of global politics'.

2 Wilhelm von Humboldt, 'On the Historian's Task', *History and Theory*, Vol. 6. No. 1 (1967), p. 57.

3 Anthony A. Bennett, *Caligula: The Corruption of Power*, New Haven: Yale University Press, 1990, pp. xv–xvi.

4 *Caligula: The Corruption of Power*, pp. xvi–xvii.

5 David Frum, *Trumpocracy: The Corruption of the American Republic*, New York: Harper, 2018, pp. xv–xvi.

6 Anonymous, *A Warning*, New York: Twelve, 2019, p. 1.

7 Brandon Rottinghaus and Justin S. Vaughn, 'How Does Trump Stack Up Against the Best – and Worst – Presidents?' *New York Times*, 19 February 2018 https://www.nytimes.com/interactive/2018/02/19/opinion/how-does-trump-stack-up-against-the-best-and-worst-presidents.html

8 Sean Wilentz, 'No, There is No Precedent', *Democracy: A Journal of Ideas*, No. 46, Fall 2017.

9 *Macbeth*, Act I, Scene III.

10 Trumpery, from the French *tromperie* (from *tromper*, to deceive, cheat).

11 https://firstdraftnews.org/latest/fake-news-complicated/

12 Timothy Snyder, *On Tyranny: Twenty Lessons from the Twentieth Century*, New York: Tim Duggan Books, 2017, p. 73.

13 Ron Suskind, 'Faith, Certainty and the Presidency of George W. Bush', *The New York Times Magazine*, 17 October 2004.

14 Tony Schwartz quoted by Jane Mayer in 'Donald Trump's Ghostwriter Tells All', *The New Yorker*, 25 January 2017.

15 *Washington Post*, 21 January 2017.

16 *New York Times*, 22 January 2017.

17 *Washington Post*, 22 January 2017.

18 Cited in *San Francisco Chronicle*, 23 January 2017.

19 *The Guardian*, 23 January 2017.

20 *Washington Post*, 25 January 2017.

21 https://edition.cnn.com/2020/06/10/politics/trump-campaign-cnn-poll/index.html

22 Tom Nichols, 'In Trump's world, reality is negotiable', *The Atlantic*, 13 January 2019 https://www.theatlantic.com/politics/archive/2019/01/donald-trump-rejects-expertise/579808/

23 Philip Rucker and Carol Leonnig, *A Very Stable Genius: Donald J. Trump's Testing of America*, New York: Bloomsbury, 2020, p. 191.

24 Quoted in *A Very Stable Genius*, p. 192.

25 Glenn Plaskin, 'The Playboy Interview with Donald Trump', *Playboy*, 1 March 1990.

26 Kira Hall, Donna M. Goldstein, and Matthew Bruce Ingram, 'The Hands of Donald Trump: Entertainment, Gesture, Spectacle', *HAU: Journal of Ethnographic Theory*, Vol. 6, No. 2, (2016), pp. 71–100.

27 Peter Burke, *Popular Culture in Early Modern Europe*, New York: Harper and Rowe, 1978.

28 Mikhail Bakhtin, *Rabelais and his World*, (Trans. Helene Iswolsky), Bloomington: Indiana University Press, 1984.

29 Erving Goffman, *The Presentation of Self in Everyday Life*, New York: Random House, 1959.

30 Dan P. McAdams, *The Strange Case of Donald J. Trump: A Psychological Reckoning*, New York: Oxford University Press, 2020.

31 Dan P. McAdams, 'The Mind of Donald Trump', *The Atlantic*, June 2016 https://www.theatlantic.com/magazine/archive/2016/06/the-mind-of-donald-trump/480771/

32 James Poniewozik, 'The Real Donald Trump Is a Character on TV', *New York Times*, 6 September 2019 https://www.nytimes.com/2019/09/06/opinion/sunday/trump-reality-tv.html

33 Nancy Gibbs, 'The danger of Donald Trump's ignorance', *Time*, 1 October 2019 https://time.com/5690324/donald-trump-ignorance/

34 Phillip Rucker and Carol Leonnig, *A Very Stable Genius: Donald J. Trump's Testing of America*, New York: Bloomsbury, 2020, p. 169.

35 *A Very Stable Genius*, p. 170.

36 *Twitter*, 8 June 2019.

37 *Sioux Falls Argus Leader*, 24 April 2018 https://www.argusleader.com/story/news/2018/04/24/president-donald-trump-mount-rushmore-trumpmore/544597002/

38 Christian L. Hart, 'Is President Trump an "Outliar"?' *Psychology Today*, 30 April 2020 https://www.psychologytoday.com/us/blog/the-nature-deception/202004/is-president-trump-outliar

39 Michael Gerson, 'Trump is the king of lies', *Washington Post*, 24 July 2020 https://www.washingtonpost.com/opinions/trump-is-the-king-of-lies/2020/07/23/b9a52fb0-cd02-11ea-91f1-28aca4d833a0_story.html

40 Christian Paz, 'All the President's Lies About the Coronavirus', *The Atlantic*, 17 August 2020 https://www.theatlantic.com/politics/archive/2020/08/trumps-lies-about-coronavirus/608647/

41 *The Guardian*, 'Trump says he ordered coronavirus testing to "slow down"', 21 June 2020 https://www.theguardian.com/world/2020/jun/21/global-report-trump-says-he-ordered-coronavirus-testing-to-slow-down

42 Paul Krugman, 'What You Don't Know Can't Hurt Trump', *New York Times*, 20 July 2020 https://www.nytimes.com/2020/07/20/opinion/trump-coronavirus-testing.html

43 'The danger of Donald Trump's ignorance.'

44 Francis J. Mootz III, 'Ugly American Hermeneutics', *Nevada Law Journal*, No. 10 (2009–2010) p. 587.

45 *Washington Post*, 6 November 2017.

46 Michael Lewis, *The Fifth Risk*, New York: W.W. Norton & Co., 2018, p. 29.

47 Phillip Rucker and Carol Leonnig, *A Very Stable Genius: Donald J. Trump's Testing of America,* New York: Bloomsbury, 2020, p. 163.

48 https://www.politico.com/story/2018/08/13/trump-world-knowledge-diplomatic-774801

49 https://www.politico.eu/article/donald-trump-belgium-is-a-beautiful-city-hellhole-us-presidential-election-2016-america/

50 John Bolton interview with ABC News' Martha Raddatz, 22 June 2020 https://abcnews.go.com/Politics/transcript-john-bolton-interview-abc-news-martha-raddatz/story?id=71287825

51 https://www.pewresearch.org/global/2020/01/08/trump-rat-ings-remain-low-around-globe-while-views-of-u-s-stay-most-ly-favorable/

52 Brendon O'Connor, 'Six types of ugly American, and Donald Trump is all of them', *The Conversation,* 3 November 2016. https://theconversation.com/six-types-of-ugly-american-and-donald-trump-is-all-of-them-67910

53 Chris Turner, *Planet Simpson,* London: Ebury Press, 2004, pp. 164–5.

54 *Planet Simpson,* p. 166.

55 *Guardian,* 17 June 2015 https://www.theguardian.com/us-news/2015/jun/16/donald-trump-reveals-net-worth-presiden-tial-campaign-launch

56 *Des Moines Register,* 1 June 2015 https://www.desmoinesreg-ister.com/story/news/elections/presidential/caucus/2015/06/01/donald-trump-straw-poll-mitt-romney-gucci-store/28313569/

57 Bob Woodward, *Fear: Trump in the White House,* London: Simon & Schuster, 2018, p. 43.

58 Anonymous, *A Warning,* New York: Twelve, 2019, p. 76.

59 *New York Daily News,* 5 November 2015.

60 Donald J. Trump, *Crippled America: How to Make America Great Again,* New York: Threshold, 2015.

61 *The Economist,* 5 September 2015.

62 Michael D'Antonio, *Never Enough: Donald Trump and the Pursuit of Success,* New York: Thomas Dunne Books, 2015, p. 3.

63 *Washington Post*, 26 May 2017.

64 Neil Postman, *Amusing Ourselves to Death: Public Discourse in the Age of Show Business*, London: Penguin (2005 ed.), p. 126.

65 Daniel J. Boorstin, *The Image: A Guide to Pseudo-events in America*, New York: Atheneum, 1971 ed.

66 Deborah L. Madsen, *American Exceptionalism*, Jackson: University Press of Mississippi, 1998, p. 1.

67 Lee Harris, *The Next American Civil War: The Populist Revolt Against the Liberal Elite*, New York: Palgrave Macmillan, 2010, p. 41.

68 Margaret MacMillan, *Peacemakers: The Paris Conference of 1919 and its Attempt to End War*, London: J. Murray, 2001, p. 22.

69 Alexis de Tocqueville, *Democracy in America*, (Trans. Gerald E. Bevan), Vol. 2, Part 1, Ch. 9, London: 2003, p. 525.

70 Seymour Martin Lipset, *American Exceptionalism: A Double-Edged Sword*, New York: W. W. Norton & Co., 1996, p. 18.

71 Seymour Martin Lipset, *The First New Nation: The United Nations in Historical and Comparative Perspective*, New York: Basic Books, 1963.

72 Richard Hofstadter, *Anti-Intellectualism in American Life*, New York: Alfred A. Knopf, 1964, p. 145.

73 *The Next American Civil War*, p. 50.

74 https://wzb.eu/system/files/docs/sv/iuk/Katzenstein_wm164.pdf

75 Joseph Nye, Jr., 'American exceptionalism in the Age of Trump', *The Strategist* (Australian Strategic Policy Institute, 12 June 2010 https://www.aspistrategist.org.au/american-exceptionalism-in-the-age-of-trump/

76 Joseph S. Nye, Jr., *Do Morals Matter: Presidents and Foreign Policy from FDR to Trump*, New York: Oxford University Press, 2020.

77 David Corn, 'Trump Says He Doesn't Believe in "American Exceptionalism"', *Mother Jones*, 7 June 2016 https://www.motherjones.com/politics/2016/06/donald-trump-american-exceptionalism/

78 James Truslow Adams, *The Epic of America*, Boston: Little, Brown, 1931.

79 *Forbes*, 22 May 2007.

80 *The Economist*, 5 September 2015.

81 Leo Hindery, Jr. and Rick Sloan, 'We must reject Trump's coup on the American Dream', *The Hill*, 20 February 2020 https://thehill.com/opinion/civil-rights/483935-we-must-reject-trumps-coup-on-the-american-dream

82 Interview with Joe Kernan on CNBC's *Squark Box*, 11 April 2019 https://www.cnbc.com/2019/04/11/mike-pence-says-the-american-dream-was-dying-until-trump-was-inaugurated.html

83 Chris Hedges and Joe Sacco, *Days of Destruction, Days of Revolt*, New York: Nation Books, 2012, pp. 226–7.

84 https://www.realclearpolitics.com/docs/190305_RCOR_Topline_V2.pdf

85 'Has Donald Trump Influenced the American Dream?' *U. S. Business News*, 30 April 2020 https://www.usbusiness-news.com/2020-has-donald-trump-influenced-the-american-dream

86 Michael D'Antonio, *Never Enough: Donald Trump and the Pursuit of Success*, New York: Thomas Dunne Books, 2015, p. 335.

87 Aristotle, *The Politics*, (Trans. T. A. Sinclair), Book IV Ch. X Harmondsworth: Penguin, 1962.

88 Sean Illing, 'The people's tyrant: what Plato can teach us about Donald Trump', *Vox*, 7 November 2016 https://www.vox.com/policy-and-politics/2016/11/7/13512960/donald-trump-plato-democracy-tyranny-fascism-2016-elections

89 Plato, *The Republic*, (Trans. H. D. P. Lee), Part IV, Book VIII, Harmondsworth: Penguin, 1955.

90 See George Grote, *A History of Greece: from the Earliest Period to the Close of the Generation Contemporary with Alexander the Great*, London: John Murray, (1888 ed.), 10 v.

91 David F. Clifton, 'Make Athens Great Again!', *The Harvard Crimson*, 1 March 2017, https://www.thecrimson.com/article/2017/3/1/clifton-make-athens-great/

92 *The Hollywood Reporter*, 3 April 2013, https://www.holly-

woodreporter.com/thr-esq/donald-trump-withdraws-bill-ma-her-432675

93 'Make Athens Great Again!'

94 Suetonius, *Caligula*, (Trans. Robert Graves), London: Penguin, 2015, p. 20.

95 *Caligula*, p. 31.

96 *Caligula*, p. 36.

97 Xavier Marquez, 'Why Trump administration officials try so hard to flatter him', *Washington Post*, 10 January 2018 https://www.washingtonpost.com/news/monkey-cage/wp/2018/01/10/why-trump-administration-officials-try-so-hard-to-flatter-him/

98 *Caligula*, p. 38.

99 Michael Wolff, *Fire and Fury: Inside the Trump White House*, London: Little, Brown, 2018, p. 23.

100 *Caligula*, p. 21.

101 Cassius Dio, *Roman History*, (Trans.by Earnest Cary, Herbert B. Foster), Vol VII, Book LIX, *Loeb Classical Library edition*, Cambridge, MA: Harvard University Press, 1924.

102 'Donald Trump: "I am the Chosen One"', *Premier Christian News*, 22 August 2019 https://premierchristian.news/en/news/article/donald-trump-i-am-the-chosen-one

103 'Donald Trump: 'I am the Chosen One.''

104 *USA Today*, 25 November 2019 https://www.usatoday.com/story/news/politics/2019/11/25/rick-perry-trump-gods-chosen-one/4295185002/

105 Chris Cillizza, 'Yes. Donald Trump really believes he is the chosen one', 24 August 2019 https://edition.cnn.com/2019/08/21/politics/donald-trump-chosen-one/index.html

106 Donald J. Trump (with Tony Schwartz), *Trump: The Art of the Deal*, London: Penguin (2016 edition), p. 58.

107 *Washington Post*, 2 June 2020.

108 *New York Times*, 2 June 2020.

109 Citizens for Responsibility in Ethics in Washington (CREW) https://www.citizensforethics.org/2000-trump-con-

flics-of-interest-counting/

110 *Caligula*, p. 43.

111 *Caligula*, pp. 43–4.

112 Rick Reilly, *Commander in Cheat: How Golf Explains Trump*, New York: Hachette Books, 2019.

113 'The Italian Bob', originally aired 1 December 2005, https://simpsonswiki.com/wiki/Benito_Mussolini

114 Jonathan Blitzer, 'A Scholar of Fascism Sees a Lot That's Familiar with Trump', *New Yorker*, 4 November 2016.

115 Ruth Ben-Ghiat, 'An American Authoritarian', *The Atlantic*, 10 August 2016, https://www.theatlantic.com/politics/archive/2016/08/american-authoritarianism-under-donald-trump/495263/

116 *Washington Post*, 29 February 2016.

117 Madeleine Albright, *Fascism: A Warning*, William Collins, London, 2018, p. 24,

118 *Salt Lake Tribune*, 13 February 2020, https://www.sltrib.com/opinion/commentary/2020/02/13/joe-jarvis-yes-stewart/

119 *The Hill*, 25 October 2019 https://thehill.com/blogs/blog-briefing-room/news/467551-retired-four-star-general-blasts-white-house-over-nytimes

120 Quote attributed to Juan Antonio Ansaldo, monarchist and aviator, cited in Tatjana Pavlovic, *Despotic Bodies and Transgressive Bodies: Spanish Culture from Francisco Franco to Jesus Franco*, New York: SUNY Press, 2002, p. 20.

121 *New York Times*, 9 August 2016.

122 *Salon*, 18 September 2015. https://www.salon.com/test2/2015/09/18/donald_trump_were_going_to_be_looking_at_how_to_get_rid_of_muslims_and_foreigners_like_obama/

123 Frank Dikötter, *The Cultural Revolution: A People's History 1962-1976*, London: Bloomsbury, 2016, p. xiii.

124 *Vanity Fair*, 1 May 2020 https://www.vanityfair.com/news/2020/05/donald-trump-called-armed-right-wing-protesters-good-people

125 Cited in Roderick McFarquar and Michael Schoenhals,

Mao's Last Revolution, Cambridge, Mass.: Belknap Press of Harvard University Press, 2006.

126 *Washington Post*, 16 March 2016.

127 Gino Spocchia, 'Trump said in 2014 riots would fix economic crash and return country to "when we were great"', *The Independent*, 2 June 2020 https://www.independent.co.uk/news/world/americas/us-politics/trump-riots-fox-news-obamacare-putin-economy-us-coronavirus-george-floyd-a9544491.html

128 *New York Times*, 1 June 2020.

129 Quoted in Phillip Rucker and Carol Leonnig, *A Very Stable Genius: Donald J. Trump's Testing of America*, New York: Bloomsbury, 2020, p. 165.

130 Anonymous (A senior Trump Administration official), *A Warning*, London: Little Brown, 2019, p. 63.

131 Cited in Michael Wolff, *Fire and Fury: Inside the Trump White House*, London: Little, Brown, p. 49.

132 See https://moralfoundations.org/

133 Gregg R. Murray, 'Is Trump a tyrant? What his tweets say', *Psychology Today*, 12 June 2016, https://www.psychologytoday.com/au/blog/caveman-politics/201606/is-trump-tyrant-what-his-tweets-say

134 Charles Blow, 'Obama Lives in Trump's Head', *New York Times*, 17 May 2017, https://www.nytimes.com/2020/05/17/opinion/trump-obama.html

135 William B. Bonvillian, 'US manufacturing decline and the rise of new production innovation paradigms', OECD, https://www.oecd.org/industry/us-manufacturing-decline-and-the-rise-of-new-production-innovation-paradigms.htm#:~:text=Between%202000%20and%202010%2C%20US,-just%2012.3%20million%20in%202016)

136 John B. Judis, *The Populist Explosion: How the Great Recession Transformed American and European Politics*, New York: *Columbia Global Reports*, 2016, p. 75.

137 *The Populist Explosion*, p. 75.

138 Norman Abjorensen, 'Donald Trump the genius? Democ-

racy struggling to find its place after the outsider rewrote its 'rules',' *Sydney Morning Herald*, 31 March 2017, https://www.smh.com.au/opinion/donald-trump-the-genius-democracy-struggling-to-find-its-place-after-the-outsider-rewrote-its-rules-20170331-gvbdiy.html

139 https://www.pewresearch.org/politics/2016/08/18/clinton-trump-supporters-have-starkly-different-views-of-a-changing-nation/

140 Andrew McGill, 'Hope is what separates Trump voters from Clinton voters, *The Atlantic*, 19 August 2016, https://www.theatlantic.com/politics/archive/2016/08/donald-trump-manu-facturing-jobs-hope/496541/

141 Michael Wolff, *Fire and Fury: Inside the Trump White House*, London: Little, Brown, 2018, p. 23.

142 Alan Abramovitz, *The Great Alignment: Race, Party Transfor-mation, and the Rise of Donald Trump*. New Haven: Yale Univer-sity Press, 2018, p. 123.

143 Jacob Pramuk, 'Trump: 'President Barack Obama was born in the United States. Period.'' *CNBC News*, 16 September 2016, https://www.cnbc.com/2016/09/16/trump-president-obama-was-born-in-the-united-states-period.html

144 Federal Election Commission, Official 2016 Presidential General Election Results, https://transition.fec.gov/pubrec/fe2016/2016presgeresults.pdf

145 *New York Times*, 28 November 2016.

146 https://www.wnyc.org/story/new-york-lawmak-ers-skip-out-trumps-inauguration/

147 *A Very Stable Genius*, p. 27.

148 See Steve Eder & Dave Philipps, 'Donald Trump's Draft Deferments: Four for College, One for Ba Feet', *New York Times*, 1 August 2016, https://www.nytimes.com/2016/08/02/us/politics/donald-trump-draft-record.html; Steve Eder, 'Did a Queens Podiatrist Help Donald Trump Avoid Vietnam?' *New York Times*, 26 December 2018 https://www.nytimes.com/2018/12/26/us/politics/trump-vietnam-draft-exemption.html

149 John G. Hubbell, *P.O.W.: A Definitive History of the American Prisoner-Of-War Experience in Vietnam, 1964–1973*, New York: Reader's Digest Press, 1976, pp. 363–4.

150 Robert Timberg, *John McCain: An American Odyssey*, New York: Touchstone Books, 1999, p. 89.

151 Todd Purdum, 'Prisoner of Conscience', *Vanity Fair*, February 2007.

152 Address to Iowa Family Summit, 18 July 2015.

153 Michael Wolff, *Siege: Trump Under Fire*, London: Little, Brown, 2019, p. 223.

154 *CNN News*, 26 August 2018.

155 *Washington Post*, 27 August 2018.

156 Peter Baker, 'In McCain Memorial Service, Two Presidents Offer Tribute, and a Contrast to Trump', *New York Times*, 1 September 2018 https://www.nytimes.com/2018/09/01/us/politics/ john-mccain-funeral.html

157 *New York Times*, 1 September 2018.

158 Maggie Haberman, Annie Karni and Michael Tackett, 'Months After John McCain's Death, Trump Keeps Feud With Him Alive', *New York Times*, 20 March 2019 https://www.ny- times.com/2019/03/20/us/politics/trump-john-mccain.html

159 Chris Sommerfeldt, 'Trump falsely claims he "had to approve" John McCain's funeral, complains he didn't get a "thank you"', *New York Daily News*, 20 March 2019 https:// www.nydailynews.com/news/politics/ny-trump-falsely-ap- prove-mccain-thank-you-20190320-bpysi4urmvae7jlqolk- w4o6a34-story.html

160 *New York Daily News*, 20 March 2019.

161 *A Warning*, pp. 3–5.

162 Interview in *Vanity Fair*, 17 August 2016.

163 Jessica Mathews, 'What Trump is Throwing Out the Win- dow', *New York Review of Books*, 9 February 2017.

164 *The Guardian*, 19 April 2019.

165 *A Warning*, p. 174.

166 *A Warning*, pp. 175–6.

167 President Trump ordering the assassination of the Syrian president and his leadership team, quoted in Bob Woodward, *Fear: Trump in the White House*, London: Simon & Schuster, 2018, p. 147.

168 Anonymous, *A Warning*, New York: Twelve, 2019, p. 149.

169 Michael Wolff, *Fire and Fury: Inside the Trump White House*, *London:* Little, Brown, 2018, p. 156.

170 Michael Wolff, *Siege: Trump Under Fire*, London: Little, Brown, 2019, p. 16.

171 *A Warning*, p. 38.

172 *USA Today*, 29 March 2017.

173 *The New Republic*, 29 August 2019.

174 Quoted in Phillip Rucker and Carol Leonnig, *A Very Stable Genius: Donald J. Trump's Testing of America*, New York: Bloomsbury, 2020, p. 165.

175 *A Warning*, p. 28.

176 *A Warning*, p. 48,

177 *New York Times*, 7 April 2020.

178 *Washington Post*, 16 May 2020.

179 *Dallas News*, 7 December 2018.

180 *Fear*, p. 54.

181 *A Very Stable Genius*, pp. 135–6.

182 *A Very Stable Genius*, p. 138.

183 Bob Woodward, *Fear: Trump in the White House*, London: Simon & Schuster, 2018, p. 226.

184 *Fear*, p. 287.

185 'Tillerson reveals frustrations about Kushner working behind his back', *CNN News*, 27 June 2019 https://edition.cnn.com/2019/06/27/politics/tillerson-kushner-frustrations/index.html

186 Quoted in *Washington Post*, 8 December 2018.

187 *Dallas News*, 7 December 2018.

188 *A Very Stable Genius*, p. 15.

189 *Fear*, p. 18.

190 *Fear*, p. 144.

191 *Fear*, p. 145.

192 *A Very Stable Genius*, p. 145.

193 *Fire and Fury*, p. 235.

194 Molly Ball, 'The Final Humiliation of Reince Priebus', *The Atlantic*, 30 July 2017 https://www.theatlantic.com/politics/archive/2017/07/the-final-humiliation-of-reince-priebus/535368/

195 *Fear*, p. 237.

196 *Fire and Fury*, pp. 287–8.

197 *Fear*, p. 235.

198 *Fire and Fury*, pp. 281–6.

199 *Fire and Fury*, p. 289.

200 *Fire and Fury*, pp. 290.

201 Niall Stanage, 'The Memo: Kelly said to be losing influence with Trump, *The Hill*, 18 May 2018 https://thehill.com/home-news/administration/381713-the-memo-kelly-said-to-be-losing-influence-with-trump

202 *New York Times*, 8 December 2018.

203 Quoted in *Fear*, p. 87.

204 *Fear*, p. 89.

205 *A Very Stable Genius*, p. 164.

206 *Fire and Fury*, p. 192.

207 *Fear*, pp. 145–6.

208 *A Very Stable Genius*, p. 167.

209 *USA Today*, 22 March 2018.

210 *Fire and Fury*, p. 304.

211 *A Very Stable Genius*, p. 15.

212 Thomas E. Ricks, 'Mattis as defense secretary: What it means for us, for the military and for Trump', *Foreign Policy*, 26 December 2017.

213 *Fear*, p. 147.

214 Jeffrey Goldberg, 'The man who couldn't take it any more', *The Atlantic*, October 2019 https://www.theatlantic.com/magazine/archive/2019/10/james-mattis-trump/596665/

215 Full text published in *New York Times*, 20 December 2018 https://www.nytimes.com/2018/12/20/us/politics/letter-jim-mattis-trump.html

216 *New York Time s*, 23 December 2018.

217 *The Atlantic*, 4 June 2020.

218 *Fire and Fury*, p. 143.

219 Fear, xviii.

220 *Fear*, p. 158.

221 *Jewish Journal*, 25 August 2017.

222 CNBC, 6 March 2018,.

223 *Fear*, p. 2.

224 *Fire and Fury*, p. 5.

225 *Fire and Fury*, p. 31.

226 *Fire and Fury*, p. 32.

227 Joshua Green, *Devil's Bargain: Steve Bannon, Donald Trump, and the Storming of the Presidency*, London: Scribe, 2017.

228 *Devil's Bargain*, p. i.

229 *Washington Post*, 18 August 2017.

230 *New York Times*, 12 August 2017.

231 *New York Times*, 14 August 2017

232 http://www.naacp.org/latest/naacp-condemns-unite-the-right-hate-rally-in-charlottesville-virginia/

233 *New York Times*, 18 August 2017.

234 *Fire and Fury*, p. 5.

235 *Washington Examiner*, 20 September 2018.

236 *New York Times*, 8 May 2018.

237 *New York Times*, 7 January 2018.

238 *New York Times*, 28 May 2019.

239 *USA Today*, 10 September 2019.

240 John Bolton, *The Room Where it Happened: A White House Memoir*, New York: Simon & Schuster, 2020.

241 John Bolton interview with ABC News' Martha Raddatz, 22 June 2020 https://abcnews.go.com/Politics/transcript-john-bolton-interview-abc-news-martha-raddatz/story?id=71287825

242 *Politico*, 23 June 2020 https://www.politico.com/news/2020/06/23/trump-bolton-book-335089

243 George Packer, 'The President Is Winning His War on American Institutions: How Trump is destroying the civil service and bending the government to his will', *The Atlantic*, April, 2020.

Index

About the author

Norman Abjorensen formerly taught at the Australian National University, Canberra, from where he obtained a PhD for a dissertation on political leadership. He has also taught at the University of Canberra and at universities in Japan, China and the Philippines. He was Honorary Research Fellow at the Prime Ministers Centre, Museum of Australian Democracy, Old Parliament House, Canberra, 2010–13.

He is a prominent media commentator on politics and is a former journalist having been national editor of the *Sydney Morning Herald* and political editor of the *Sunday Herald*. He also held senior positions at the ABC, SBS, the *Age* and *Canberra Times*. He is the author of *John Hewson: A Biography* (1993); *Leadership and the Liberal Revival: Bolte, Askin and the Post-war Ascendancy* (2007); *John Howard and the Conservative Tradition* (2008); *The Culture Wars: Australian and American Politics in the 21st Century* (with Jim George and Kim Huynh) (2009); *Australia: The State of Democracy* (with Marian Sawer and Phil Larkin) (2009); the *Historical Dictionary of Australia* (4th ed. with James Docherty) (2014); *Combating Corruption: The G20 Action Plan and its Implications for the Asia-Pacific Region* (2015); the *Historical Dictionary of Popular Music* (2017); *The Manner of Their Going: Prime Ministerial Exits in Australia* (2015; rev. ed. 2019); and the *Historical Dictionary of Democracy* (2019)

He is currently a Visiting Fellow at the Australian National University's Crawford School of Public Policy and a Visiting Fellow at the School of Arts, Social Sciences and Humanities, Swinburne University of Technology, Melbourne.

CPSIA information can be obtained
at www.ICGtesting.com
Printed in the USA
FSHW012210091020
74632FS